CW00707956

# SOLO
# TO
# ENGLAND

## The first Tiger Moth flight
## from Australia to England

## BARRY MARKHAM

Published by

**MELROSE BOOKS**

An Imprint of Melrose Press Limited
St Thomas Place, Ely
Cambridgeshire
CB7 4GG, UK
www.melrosebooks.com

**FIRST EDITION**

Copyright © Barry Markham 2008

The Author asserts his moral right to
be identified as the author of this work

Cover created by Amanda Barrett
Based on designs by Carol Markham and Ian Pianta

**ISBN  978-1-906050-54-2**

All rights reserved. No part of this publication may be reproduced,
stored in a retrieval system, or transmitted, in any form or by any means
electronic, mechanical , photocopying, recording or otherwise,
without the prior permission of the publishers.

This book is sold subject to the condition that it shall not,
by way of trade or otherwise, be lent, re-sold, hired out or
otherwise circulated without the publisher's prior consent
in any form of binding or cover other than that in which
it is published and without a similar condition including this
condition being imposed on the subsequent purchaser.

Printed and bound in Great Britain by:
Biddles, 24 Rollesby Road, Hardwick Industrial Estate
King's Lynn. Norfolk PE30 4LS

To Carol, Campbell, Bradley, April and Alison

# PSALM 139 VERSES 9-10

*If I take the wings of the morning,*

*And dwell in the uttermost parts of the sea,*

*Even there your hand shall lead me,*

*And your right hand shall hold me.*

# FOREWORD

There is something about Moths, flying them and the men and women who fly them, that is inspirational. Barry Markham's epic trip from Langley Park to Cambridge in 60 days was certainly inspirational, made more so as it raised funds for that great Australian icon, The Royal Flying Doctor Service. What an incredible journey in *Margery* over Indonesia, Malaysia, Burma, India, Pakistan, the Middle East, Egypt, Italy and France, through 60 days and sixteen countries of incredibly testing conditions. In a way, the words painted on *Margery's* cockpit door "Walter, fly high and safe, and live your dream today" say it all and encapsulate this wonderful story and will, I believe, inspire many people to dig down deep and try to live their dreams too. All I can do, and all the people who read this book will too, is to admire Barry and be grateful to his guts and courage and to thank him for sharing this remarkable story with us.

*Henrietta Bedford*

Henrietta, Duchess of Bedford
February 2008

You may wonder why I wrote this foreword. It is one of the privileges I have in my position as President of the de Havilland Moth Club - a position I hold due to my late husband Robin's Great Grandmother, Mary - "The Flying Duchess" who also flew epic journeys.

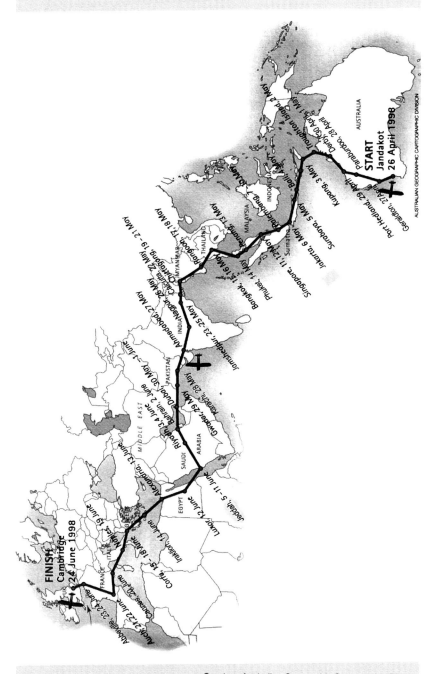

*Courtesy Australian Geographic Cartographic Division*

# CONTENTS

# INTRODUCTION

**M**y first training flight in Tiger Moth VH-FAS ('Tiger 37')
was from Jandakot Airport near Perth in May 1986.
Although I had been flying modern aircraft, such as Cessnas, for
eight years and thought I had reached a reasonable standard of
proficiency, I was in for a shock. Just taxiing was an art form,
with the nose-high attitude of the taildragger greatly limiting
forward visibility and requiring the pilot to weave from side to
side in 'S' fashion to ensure a clear path ahead. And then the take-
off roll, with head leaning out the left side of the cockpit to gain
some semblance of direction, and the sudden blast of air in the
face as the Tiger gained momentum. Once airborne, things were
relatively stable as I gradually got used to the sensitive controls of
this stick-and-rudder machine!

My interest in Tiger Moths began early. When I was a young
boy my father, Percy, often told me about his wartime experiences
of flying Tiger Moths as a RAAF trainee pilot at Cunderdin in
1943. I soon developed a strong interest in all mechanical things,
for my father at one stage had the largest collection of veteran
and vintage motor vehicles and motorcycles in the Southern
Hemisphere. I learnt to drive the majority of his cars as a young

teenager, under driving age – they included a wide range, from the humble model-T Ford to Rolls Royce Silver Ghosts and Bentleys. I also helped in the restoration of some of these vehicles. I still own a 1926 Harley Davidson which was part of his collection and on which I learnt to ride when I was fifteen.

I gained my pilot's licence at the age of thirty-four, but it was my father's good-natured ribbing that finally got me started on Tiger Moths. He used to say that although my flying achievements to that stage were commendable (e.g. night flying and aerobatics), I hadn't *really* flown until I had soloed in a Tiger Moth. My eldest brother John also flew Tiger Moths, probably for the same reason.

So the challenge was offered and I finally took it up.

Thinking back to that first flight, I can still recall the ever-tightening knot in my stomach as I contemplated landing the beast. I followed the instructor, Mike Pottier, through on the first circuit and then it was my turn. With Mike urging me to put my head further and further out of the cockpit on final approach, my eyes streaming as a result of ill-fitting goggles, and the ground looming up larger than ever, I was feeling that this was an almost impossible task I was being asked to perform. But then, with the stick held hard back into my stomach, and the forward speed of the aircraft reduced to just above the stall, the wheels touched – what a relief!

After taxiing back to the Royal Aero Club and switching off, I sat in the aircraft for a moment or two, half-stunned and half-excited. Mike climbed out first and asked, "Well, how did you enjoy that?"

Lying between my teeth I replied, "Great, can't wait for the next lesson."

But driving away from Jandakot I was in mental turmoil, wondering how I was ever going to master this cumbersome and primitive aeroplane and castigating myself for making such an open commitment to come back and have another go.

However, during the next training session it all started to come together and I drove away with a smile on my face, and this time genuinely wanting to come back and work towards my endorsement. The bug had bitten! I finally went solo after 4.4 hours and from that time on, the Tiger became my favourite flying machine.

The Tiger Moth was a thrill to fly and sitting low in the confined space of the cockpit, just 24 inches (61 centimetres) wide, shoulders almost touching each side, helped create the feeling of being one with the machine. This no doubt improved confidence and resulted in a smoother flying performance, but as even the most seasoned Tiger pilot would attest, it is an aircraft that can 'bite' or easily embarrass a pilot unless total concentration is maintained throughout every phase of the flight – from swinging the propeller to putting it away in the hangar.

The Tiger Moth biplane was developed by the de Havilland Aircraft Company as a primary trainer for the Royal Air Force (RAF) and was first flown by test pilot, Hubert Broad, on 26 October 1931. It was given the manufacturer's designation DH82. The engine was an inverted four-cylinder type known as the Gipsy III with a capacity of 5.71 litres and rated at 120hp (horsepower). Improvements to this engine soon followed with the development of the Gipsy Major I engine which had a 6.12 litre capacity and was rated at 130hp. (A Canadian built variant of this engine, known as the Gipsy Major IC, was rated at 145hp.) With the improved engine and other refinements the Tiger Moth was given the designation DH82A in 1934.

Airframe and wing construction consisted of a fabric-covered, tubular steel frame fuselage, 23 feet 11 inches (7.29 metres) in length, and two sets of timber-framed, fabric-covered wings providing a wing span of 29 feet 4 inches (8.94 metres). The open cockpits were in tandem and flown solo from the rear cockpit only, owing to centre-of-gravity limitations – instructors or passengers occupied the front seat.

Between 1931 and 1945 an estimated 8,800 Tiger Moths were produced of which 1,085 were constructed in Australia from September 1939 to August 1945. Some 600 airworthy examples survive in the world today including over 200 in Australia.

Once I'd learnt to fly a Tiger Moth it seemed a natural extension of my youthful interest in old vehicles to want to own one, and I purchased Tiger Moth A17-757 as a basket case in 1988. It was the third-to-last Tiger Moth built in Australia during the Second World War and was delivered to the RAAF at Mascot in January 1945. In 1950 it was purchased by the Royal Newcastle Aero Club (registration VH-RNQ) but, following an accident in 1959, was deregistered, dismantled and put into storage until I bought it many years later.

Ray Windred, from Luskintyre in the Hunter Valley in NSW, restored her over a four-year period. It was a ground-up restoration with all components, including the engine, fuselage and flying surfaces being either restored or replaced. The only non-standard items were the fitting of a tail wheel and brakes to comply with licensed airport requirements, radio, transponder – a radio receiving and transmitting device primarily used by Air Traffic Controllers for radar tracking purposes, GPS (global positioning system) and alternator to charge the battery. In all other respects, including the engine (Gipsy Major IC), it was just like the war-time product and it flew and handled the same. The final cost was A$85,000.

Under her new registration, VH-NOV, I flew my now pristine machine, resplendent in post-war training colours of all-over silver with yellow bands and red, white and blue roundels, solo back to Perth in October 1992.

The trip took eight days in all and 29 flying hours. It was

my greatest adventure to date. When I landed at Jandakot Airport in Perth on 17 October 1992 I had the feeling that I could just keep going and going. I was in the groove and loving it. Crossing the Great Dividing Range in northern NSW, travelling low along the cliffs of the Great Australian Bight and flying over the vast and remote Nullarbor Plain are vivid memories. It was this experience that sowed the seed to undertake a much longer and more challenging journey one day. I couldn't get the thought out of my mind and spent the next six years dreaming about a transcontinental flight.

In February 1997, I obtained my Command Instrument Rating (single engine) and although I did not continue to pursue this form of flying, the discipline learned of flying solely on instruments for extended periods of time, would later hold me in good stead.

* * *

There is nothing remarkable about my life. At the time of my trip I was fifty, married with four children and two grandchildren. I was educated at Wesley College in Perth and attended university part-time well into my adulthood. I obtained a Bachelor of Business degree and concluded with a Master of Education degree from the University of Western Australia at the age of forty-four. I run a small real estate agency founded by my late father after the war, and apart from my family, whom I cherish, my recreational time is mainly spent flying my Tiger Moth.

I'd had an enjoyable and happy life, but there was a part of me that was unfulfilled. I felt a burning desire to extend myself physically and mentally as the aviators of the 1920s and 1930s had done. I couldn't rest until this desire was satisfied. Time was running out – I had to undertake an adventure soon if I were ever going to do so.

In completing the Australia to England trip I achieved my dream. And in doing so, my outlook on life changed forever. I had overcome fear in the face of danger to an extent never experienced in my life before. I had learned to live with a nagging knot in my stomach and the fear of the unknown for the majority of the journey. These fears did not spoil the trip in any way, they were necessary components of the adventure and what I had secretly been yearning for.

# Chapter 1

## THE PLAN IS HATCHED

After I'd flown my restored Tiger Moth across Australia the years ticked away while I contemplated what adventure I should undertake and how, and when, I should embark on it. I read the accounts of famous aviators such as Sir Francis Chichester, Sir Alan Cobham, Jimmy Mollison, Bert Hinkler, Dolores Bonney, Jean Batten and Jimmy Woods for inspiration. Brian Edwards' story of his solo flight from England to Australia in a Tiger Moth in 1990 added further impetus. I was also aware that David Cyster, an Englishman, had been the first person to undertake this same flight (England to Australia) in a Tiger Moth in 1978.

However, it was reading *Jimmy Woods, Flying Pioneer* by Julie Lewis that finally decided me. All along I had wanted my flight to be something different, and here was another Perth man who had excelled as a pilot in the 1920s and 30s and obviously had the true spirit of adventure. Amongst his many flying feats was a solo flight in a Gipsy Moth from Perth to England in 1933. If I could successfully complete a similar flight, then in a sense, it would be a commemoration of Jimmy Woods' flight, but it would also be the first Tiger Moth to fly from Australia to England.

For me, the key to being different was to be flying a Tiger Moth in the reverse direction. Apart from being against the prevailing winds, I believe there was nothing inherently difficult about flying in this direction compared with those who had flown the other way (England to Australia). Although I have yet to fly a Gipsy Moth, a civilian, two seat biplane that preceded the Tiger Moth, from speaking to others who have flown both aircraft types, including over long distances, there is not a great deal of difference.

The Gipsy Moth was a popular choice amongst long-distance, solo aviators of the 1920s and 30s, primarily on account of its reliability, the availability of spares, and a number of RAF bases located along the route between Great Britain and Australia to undertake running repairs, e.g. in the Middle East and South-East Asia.

The Tiger Moth and Gipsy Moth have the same length, although the Gipsy Moth has a slightly wider wingspan. The Gipsy Moth has a cleaner airflow with the wing ribs running parallel to the fuselage, whilst the Tiger Moth's upper and lower wings are swept (the upper more than the lower) and hence the wing ribs are offset to the airflow. As a result, the Gipsy Moth is said to be a little softer, or lighter, on the controls. Further, because the Tiger Moth's upper and lower wings are staggered, they cannot be folded, whereas the Gipsy Moth's can.

In comparing engine performances, the Gipsy I engine fitted to the Gipsy Moth DH60G, for example, has a rated horsepower of 100, whereas the DH82A Tiger Moth's engine has a rated horsepower of 130 (Gipsy Major I) or 145hp (high compression Gipsy Major IC). The Gipsy Moth achieves 70 knots at 1850 cruising RPM whereas the Tiger Moth achieves 70 knots at 1950 cruising RPM (i.e. for both 130hp and 145hp types). Cockpit comfort, layout and controls are similar in both aircraft, although the inverted engine of the Tiger Moth provides better forward visibility. The main fuel tank capacity for both is the same at 19 imperial gallons or 86 litres.

There were nagging doubts. Was I too old? Was I competent enough? How would I go about planning the flight? What would it cost? And a myriad of other questions. Having kept it to myself and my family for so long, I now had to bring it out into the open and obtain some answers from the right people. As my wife Carol said to me, "You've talked about it for so long, if you are going to do it, just do it!"

So I arranged a meeting with Werner Buhlmann, a well-respected flying instructor and long-standing friend of mine. He had already undertaken several long-distance solo flights, including crossing Australia in a Tiger Moth, and flights to and from Europe in modern aircraft. From our meeting in a suburban coffee shop in 1997 things snowballed, and in a very short time, a support committee was formed comprising Gerry Gannon, a media consultant; Murray Bow, a flying instructor; Werner and myself. Having harboured this secret goal of mine for so long, with only my immediate family knowing, it was a relief to finally bring it out into the open.

Outside this committee, one of the first people I discussed my proposed trip with was Brian Edwards, who'd done the same trip but starting from England. He was very supportive and offered to assist me in whatever way he could, including the generous offer of a loan of his long-range fuel and oil tank systems. Brian also offered me sensible advice on such matters as fuel management, drinking ample water – particularly in the tropics – and perhaps most importantly, to remain in total command of the situation no matter what.

Fellow Tiger Moth enthusiast, John Fisher from NSW, was another person who gave me invaluable advice and assistance. He had flown his Tiger over a route similar to Brian Edwards'

(England to Australia) in 1996. His assistance was also very generous and included consular information, details of preferred landing points, fuel availability and advice on safety equipment, windscreen modification, seating and clothing.

Early in the planning stages I decided to involve a worthwhile charity, and to this end, I approached the Royal Flying Doctor Service of Australia, (WA Division). As an RFDS executive said at the time, although any funds raised would be very welcome, perhaps, even more importantly, the trip could be used to raise a greater awareness of the organisation and the unique services it provides.

I obtained US military charts from an Eastern States supplier covering the whole of the proposed route (some 26 in all) and detailed flight planning was undertaken with the assistance of a computer package provided by Rob Slater of Champagne PC Services (one of my first sponsors). The choice of suitable landing points and alternates was a crucial part of the planning. The aim, of course, was to take the shortest practical route and with the least number of stops. Obvious limiting factors were the range and speed of the aircraft in its trip configuration, the countries that would permit me to fly through their air space and land, and the availability of suitable airports and landing strips.

In its standard form, a Tiger Moth will cruise at around an indicated speed of 70 knots but, with 316 litres of fuel on board (instead of the standard 86 litres) the excessive weight would mean that, for approximately the first two to three hours of any flight, it would be much slower. The fuel burn rate adopted for flight planning purposes was 32 litres per hour. The prospect of encountering strong headwinds had to also be considered. For example, an aircraft with an indicated airspeed of 70 knots and a headwind of 20 knots (on the nose) is only travelling at 50 knots over the ground (called ground speed). Therefore, it was decided to plan the entire trip with a ground speed of just 50 knots, which

I hoped would be the worst-case scenario. I therefore determined that there would be a total of 35 legs (35 days of flying) and for each of those days, I prepared a separate plastic envelope containing every piece of essential information to successfully complete the flight for that day.

I spent numerous hours on the navigation charts alone – drawing in tracks, writing down radio frequencies and airport information. Werner Buhlmann helped greatly with the overall planning, as did my secretary Sunny Phegan and another friend, John Roberts. My wife Carol, being the neat and methodical person I am not, did a magnificent job in assisting to cut down the navigation charts to a more manageable size and then pack and label the thirty-five daily envelopes. The charts were cut into long strips approximately 16cm wide, with the tracks drawn in a well defined black line down the middle. This provided a visual navigation reference of about 60 nautical miles (NM) either side of track (1 nautical mile = 1.852km or 1.151 statute miles). Each chart was then carefully folded so that it would fit neatly into my velcro-fixed knee pad and could be unfolded and rotated as needed.

For flight planning purposes UTC (Coordinated Universal Time) would be used throughout the entire trip. It is the universal standard for civil time keeping using atomic clocks, and hence, forms the basis for international flight planning. UTC replaced GMT (Greenwich Mean Time) which was based on celestial standards. However, for practical purposes, I also had to be aware of the local time at each landing point, particularly as I would be travelling through sixteen countries. I would use local time for general day to day living – just as at home. I soon became adept at mentally interchanging between the two systems.

Overflight and landing clearances for the many countries I would traverse was another crucial matter. Mike Gray from Overflight International, situated on the Isle of Man, specialises in organising such clearances for international flights and, for a modest fee, did a magnificent job. However, once I had reached Egypt his services would cease and it would be left to me to obtain any further clearances required for the remainder of the trip. The reason given for this was that air-traffic authorities in the remaining countries were easier to deal with and I would not have to face the considerable red-tape that existed in South-East Asian countries in particular, as well as the language problems.

I continued to seek sponsorship and I knew from the outset this was not going to be an easy task. In all, there ended up being thirteen sponsors with the four major ones being Australian Geographic, Malaysia Airlines, Cox Aviation Insurers and Stirling Besso Ltd – Lloyd's Brokers. The others were my sister and brother-in-law, June and John Brearley; Les, Pat and Peter Gunzburg; Mountain Designs Perth; Mobil Oil; Western Automotive Pty Ltd; Skycraft Electronics; Champagne PC Services; Burns Sieber Accountants; and Old Wesley Collegians Association. The funds or goods and services received in lieu, thereof, accounted for approximately 15 percent of the total cost of the trip. The remainder was personally funded, but I will always be grateful to the sponsors who supported me.

I wanted to set a departure date early in the piece so that all planning could be carefully programmed and a reliable timetable drawn up. I decided on March/April 1998, for that would leave sufficient time to complete preparations and would also be a suitable weather window, avoiding the annual wet season of the Kimberley Region, which usually finishes in March, and the onset of the monsoon season in South-East Asia, which begins towards the end of May. Finally, 26 April was set as the departure date. In hindsight, I should have departed several weeks earlier, as I was to discover the monsoon season had already begun in South-East Asia, i.e. from Indonesia through to Myanmar (Burma) and Bangladesh.

Preparing and fitting out the Tiger for the long journey

was the most important job to get under way. I started with the engine in August 1997. The whole top end of the motor, including cylinders, heads, rocker gear and pistons, as well as both magnetos and the carburettor, were sent to Vintage Engine Technology Ltd (Vintech) in England for a complete overhaul. Vintech are considered the leaders in their field worldwide and I was most grateful to Mike Vaisey and Paul Sharman for an excellent job done in a very short turn-around time.

The Royal Aero Club of WA, based at Jandakot Airport, were assigned the task of preparing the Tiger totally, including reassembly of the engine, installation of long-range fuel and oil tank and transfer systems, additional compass, GPS, new tyres and an enlarged perspex windshield. There were four fuel tanks in all – the existing main tank (86.3 litres) located between the two upper wings, existing auxiliary tank (45.4 litres) located in the forward section of the front cockpit, ferry fuel tank No. 1 (150 litres) located in the main section of the front cockpit where the passenger's seat had been removed, and ferry tank No. 2 (35 litres) which sat on top of ferry tank No. 1. The existing oil tank held 9 litres and a ferry oil tank positioned next to ferry fuel tank No. 2, 7 litres. The front windscreen was removed and a cockpit cover made from thin ply-wood fitted neatly over the front cockpit opening. This cover concealed the ferry and auxiliary tanks and ensured a smooth air-flow over this section of the fuselage.

Work commenced early in January 1998 culminating with a test flight with the Tiger in full ferry configuration (i.e. equipped with long-range fuel tanks) on 21 March. A final full load check involving a staged climb to 9,000 feet was made on 1 April. Extras on the aircraft included a life raft (my seat), tool kit and two small boxes of spare parts. All hangar personnel involved did a marvellous job and I had every confidence my machine could last the distance.

Fuel and oil burn rates were monitored on this and subsequent flights, and CASA (Civil Aviation Safety Authority) required a log to be kept of the oil burn rate for the first 20 hours. As I expected, the engine bedded in beautifully and I finished up with a brilliant burn rate of 1 litre per 8 hours.

With an anticipated total flight time of between 175 and 200 hours, it was clear that the minimum mandatory servicing required en route would include a 50-hour service followed by a 100-hour service and then at least one further 50-hour service. As my plan from the outset was to carry out the flight without any support crew or prearranged maintenance assistance, I had to be suitably trained. Don Longville, an engineer with the Royal Aero Club of WA, gave me excellent training and after being signed out by Glen Caple, Chief Engineer at the Club, I received CASA approval. I now had a much better understanding into the workings and intricacies of the Tiger Moth.

On the matter of safety equipment, I had to choose between a parachute and a life raft as there would be insufficient room for both. This is apart from the helicopter-type life jacket I would wear whenever I was over water. I reasoned that, apart from having never made a parachute jump, a parachute on its own would be of little use if I finished up in the middle of a large expanse of water, such as the Timor Sea or the Mediterranean. I felt that I had a better chance of ditching in the water or making a forced landing on terra firma – wherever I happened to be at the time.

And so I opted for a life raft. The RAAF agreed to loan me a Macchi jet type and I underwent training in its use with a group of trainee PC9 pilots at the RAAF Air Base, Pearce, just north of Perth. I also read up on the theory of ditching and the preferred techniques for handling different wind and water conditions.

One piece of advice the RAAF instructor gave me stuck firmly in my mind. It was that when the Tiger Moth impacted the water (the contact would not be gentle) it would most likely sink quickly, and the only items I could bank on taking with me when exiting the cockpit would be what was in my hands at the time. In this case it had to be the life raft which I would be sitting on. Therefore, two webbing straps (approximately 40cm long) were attached one each side of the life raft by clip-on buckles, with the loose ends positioned near my thighs. Prior to impact, I was to grab one of these straps and not let go: The life raft would leave the aircraft with me.

A final hurdle I had to clear was to obtain special CASA approval to fly the Tiger overweight and in what was termed ferry configuration. The maximum all-up weight of my Tiger Moth in its standard form was 828kg and my planned maximum all-up weight (including the pilot and full fuel) was 910kg. Furthermore, carrying a full fuel load of 316 litres to provide a maximum endurance of 9.9 hours, meant that I would have to burn off a minimum three hours and thirty eight minutes of fuel (116 litres) after take-off before I could land again, i.e. the maximum landing weight stipulated by CASA for my planned trip was 828kg. It was considered that to land any earlier would place undue stresses on the aeroplane, and therefore be unsafe.

The decision processes of CASA were influenced by the very recent tragedy of fellow formation pilot and Club member, Bob Dalley. There appeared to have been a structural failure in one of the wings of the Tiger Bob was flying, though at that stage, the precise cause had yet to be determined. Bob was a real flying enthusiast and his passing, and the crash itself was a cause of great grief to us all. It had a particularly sobering effect on me with my planned departure date just four weeks away.

With only days to spare, CASA's approval finally came through. They had done their best to expedite the approval process in association with Aeronautical Engineers Australia and British Aerospace in England.

The final full-load check flight on 21 April, just five days prior to departure, brought home to me that this trip had now passed the planning and preparation stages and was for real. I could feel the excitement building up in me.

My Tiger now carried the name *Margery* after my late mother. She had passed away just six months previously and had always been a strong supporter of my flying. I am so thankful that I was able to tell her of my planned flight while she was alive and that I was naming the Tiger after her.

A special message was painted on the left door of my Tiger Moth to greet me each day as I climbed into the cockpit to commence the next leg. It was from my wife Carol and read –

*Walter, fly high and safe,*
*And live your dream today.*

'Walter' referred to Walter Mitty, James Thurber's fictional character who was always dreaming he was someone famous, or else a person of incredible skill and daring. For instance, a famous surgeon performing an intricate operation or a pilot flying a bomber solo through a barrage. Carol had thought for many years that my own wild dreams and fantasies were akin to Walter Mitty's and hence the nickname. She had written the message with love and it was my constant companion.

Before dressing the Tiger up in her final livery of sponsorship messages and logos, the red, white and blue RAAF roundels on the wings and fuselage were blanked out. This was for safety reasons when travelling through parts of Asia and the Middle East, where anything with foreign military connotations – even an old World War II biplane, might be considered a security risk and dealt with accordingly.

To record my trip, apart from the daily diary I would keep, I purchased a 35mm Canon A1 Sureshot underwater camera. It was compact, simple to operate and the underwater capability was chosen because of the rain I might encounter and also the humidity of the tropics, both of which I thought could affect the operation of the camera or the film itself. It almost became part of me, and the bright red strap would be slung around my neck on every leg.

One final and pleasant task to perform prior to my departure was to officially thank everyone who had assisted or supported me over the previous twelve months. On Thursday 23 April, a late afternoon tea party was held in the RFDS hangar at Jandakot Airport for this purpose and approximately sixty people were in attendance including family, friends and of course the sponsors. *Margery* was now ready to go and was parked at the entrance to the hangar in front of the assembled crowd. It was a simple but warm and friendly occasion. With only two days to go, I could now concentrate solely on the trip and take time to prepare myself mentally.

Saturday 25 April (Anzac Day), one day prior to my departure, I spent at home quietly with Carol and daughters April and Alison. Several friends rang throughout the day to wish me well, which I greatly appreciated. In the early evening I went out to Jandakot with Carol and carefully packed *Margery*. And then it was home for an early night, ready for the exciting day ahead.

# Chapter 2

# THE FLIGHT BEGINS:
# PERTH TO TROUGHTON ISLAND

**Days 1-6** - 26 April 1998 to 1 May 1998

Sunday 26 April dawned a beautiful day. I was up at 6.30am, had a quick breakfast and headed straight out to Jandakot Airport. At the hangar, I met my brother John who was going to be flying his Tiger Moth in the formation flight to the official departure point, Langley Park in Perth city. Some years ago he had acquired a twin-engined Piper Chieftain in the US and flown it back to Australia with Glen Caple, Chief Engineer of the Royal Aero Club of WA: he no doubt knew what I was feeling today. We had a good brotherly chat before carrying out the mandatory first flight, daily checks on our respective aircraft, and then went to the pilot briefing for the formation flight. The aircraft and pilots for this flight were as follows:

| No. 1 | DH82A Tiger Moth | VH-BTP | Clark Rees |
|---|---|---|---|
| No. 2 | DH82A Tiger Moth | VH-DBC | Doug Brooks |
| No. 3 | DH82A Tiger Moth (passenger Brian Edwards) | VH-NMD | John Markham |
| No. 4 | DH82A Tiger Moth | VH-BAR | Kevin Bailey |
| No. 5 | DH82A Tiger Moth | VH-NIG | Nigel Emmans |
| No. 6 | DH82A Tiger Moth | VH-WHW | Chris Boyes |
| No. 7 | DH82A Tiger Moth | VH-NOV | Barry Markham |
| No. 8 | DHC-1 Chipmunk (passenger Werner Buhlmann) | VH-RWI | Gail Neylan |
| No. 9 | DHC-1 Chipmunk | VH-FLC | Gerry Hughes |
| No. 10 | DHC-1 Chipmunk | VH-RNW | Glen Caple |
| No. 11 | DHC-1 Chipmunk | VH-LBW | Ross Campbell |

We were all members of the Royal Aero Club of WA and had flown in formation together on numerous occasions over the years, though usually in smaller numbers. I felt honoured that they had chosen to support me in this way on the day of my departure. It was also appropriate that the aircraft were Tiger Moths and Chipmunks, with the latter being a monoplane trainer, the successor to the Tiger Moth that first flew in 1946.

Mine was the last of the Tigers to land at Langley Park, followed by the Chipmunks. The assembled crowd of about 2,000 people surprised me, as did the media presence. Family, friends and neighbours were all there and I was absolutely thrilled. Following a number of media interviews, Ross Willcock, Mayor of Cambridge, Western Australia (my home district) presented me with an ornate handwritten scroll to present to the Mayor of Cambridge, England.

His Excellency, Major General Michael Jeffery, AC MC, Governor of Western Australia, then spoke briefly to the gathering about my pending flight and also had a short, friendly chat with Carol and then myself. He showed a genuine interest in what I was about to undertake and made reference to the feats of pioneer solo aviator and sailor, Sir Francis Chichester.

Frank Colquhoun, who had helped prepare Jimmy Woods' Gipsy Moth for the Australia–England flight in 1933, was also there and he offered some helpful advice on refuelling from drums, urging me to be careful of water contamination.

At noon, it was time to get ready to depart. I was worried about lifting off with all the extra weight I was carrying as there was only a light westerly breeze blowing. The crowd were ushered back behind the rope barricades leaving me just with my family, Carol, April, Alison, my son Bradley, his wife Marie and grandson Calvin. It was an emotional moment and brought home to me what a wonderful, supportive family they are.

Werner swung the propeller and the carefully prepared World War II Gipsy Major engine burst into life. The Governor dipped a large flag signalling me to taxi to the holding point at the end of the grass field. With the slats open to assist lift, I slowly opened the throttle and commenced the take-off run. With all the weight aboard, poor *Margery* was reluctant to take to the air. She settled back onto the ground twice after briefly rising and after 200 metres, the line of palm trees at the other end of the field loomed larger and larger. I gave myself another 75 metres for lift off, otherwise I would abort the take-off. The Tiger rose again about 30cm and settled slightly, but this time the wheels did not make contact. I managed to climb safely away. What a relief! I had a heartbreaking flash of the trip ending there and then with *Margery* mushing into the palm trees! I slowly circled Langley Park, at the same time gaining height and waiting for the rest of the formation to catch up.

I then headed straight for the west coast to commence my journey northwards. Brother John was flying in his Tiger in the number 3 position (to my immediate left) with Brian Edwards as passenger and it felt fitting that they were both there. Hillarys Boat Harbour stood out clearly a few miles ahead with yachts and launches tied in neat lines to their pens, and the adjoining board-walk cafes and shops. Another two miles and I was over Mullaloo Point – a sand dune and scrub-covered bump on the coast. I climbed to 2,000 feet and headed north for Geraldton, my first overnight stop. The rest of the formation headed south for Jandakot Airport and final cheerios were communicated on frequency 123.45. Now it was down to business.

I felt a little numb and fairly exhausted by the time I was left on my own. The pristine white beaches seemed to go on forever and contrasted brilliantly with the deep blue of the ocean: I always enjoyed coastal flying. With the Indian Ocean remaining constantly on my left, the trip to the coastal fishing town of Geraldton was uneventful and I managed a ground speed of 90 knots. My flight path took me just south of the town as I now headed inland in a north-easterly direction to the airport, five miles away. Low native scrub and farmlands passed beneath me and the Kojarena and Waterloo Ranges formed a backdrop to the airport, making it easier to sight. Flight time was only 3.1 hours, but it felt like enough for Day 1. What a surprise I had on landing to be greeted by three friends, Richard and Cathy McKenna from the farming town of Tardun, and Mick Harcourt, a fellow Tiger Moth enthusiast from Perth. I appreciated their support very much.

Chris Shine from Shine Aviation kindly allowed me to leave *Margery* in his hangar overnight. At the motel I rang Carol and the girls at home to let them know I was okay. I also read a farewell letter from Richard Court MLA, Premier of Western Australia, that had been handed to me just prior to my departure from Langley Park. I appreciated the gesture and was heartened by his message. My final duty for the day, as it would be for the rest of the trip, was to go over my flight plan and maps for the next day's flight. Paraburdoo, an inland mining town, was my destination and covering 378NM would be a 6-7 hour flight, my first long distance test.

I went to bed happy after a hectic and exciting day.

Early the next morning, on 27 April, I had a telephone interview with the BBC and then went out to the airport to refuel *Margery*, obtain a weather report and lodge my flight plan. The hangar was one of the original World War II hangars that housed Avro Ansons and I felt nostalgic for a moment as Dad had been based here in 1944 and had qualified on the Avro Anson as a sergeant pilot. I recalled the stories of his training, the endless hours of submarine patrols and the hardship of being separated from his family in Perth; then the hope of being posted to England upon completion of the course, which he was. Dad had passed away in 1994, three-and-a-half years prior to my departure, and I will always remember him as an intelligent, strong and dignified man. I looked up to him as a father and for his life achievements: he was a great influence in my life.

I took off just after 9.00am and at exactly 10.55am I received a few drops of rain from a solitary cloud directly above me. Approximately halfway through this leg I noticed a small vapour trail coming from the top of the fuel gauge on the main tank which sits between the two upper wings. Nothing to be overly concerned about, but I would definitely need to attend to it once on the ground.

At around midday, I started to experience turbulence as the ground beneath me was progressively heating up. It was a hot, bumpy ride for the last two-and-a-half hours into Paraburdoo, a small town of around 2,000 people, established in 1970 by Hamersley Iron to house its workers. Just a slight bounce on landing, not too hard, and upon disembarking I could feel the heat from the black tarmac. There wasn't a soul around, so I pulled *Margery* into a parking spot, chocked her and put the canvas cockpit cover on.

A large, burly figure approached from the other side of the wire mesh fence surrounding the parking area. For a moment I wasn't sure if he was friend or foe – had I parked in the wrong area? Was there something wrong with my approach and landing?

"Do you want any fuel?" he called out.

I responded in the affirmative, but that I would probably do it in the morning.

"How much do you want?" was his next question.

"About 150 litres."

"Okay, it's on me, I've got a lot of time for the RFDS". He had obviously noticed the painted logo on the engine cowl.

His name was Vince Costello and he was the proprietor of the BP fuel agency in Paraburdoo. This was a very generous gesture on his part. And it wasn't just an isolated incident, as I later found out – other people I encountered in the Pilbara and Kimberley regions were similarly friendly and generous.

I reached my motel around 4.30pm. Carol rang and told me she would meet me in Port Hedland tomorrow, together with my son Campbell, his wife, Amanda-Sue and baby Gabrielle. Campbell and Amanda-Sue were living in Roebourne, about four hours drive away, and because of distance and work commitments had been unable to be present for my departure from Perth. This would, therefore, be a great opportunity to catch up with them, for within a few days I would have left Australia behind.

On 28 April I was up at 6.15am and lodged my flight plan by telephone from the motel. Vince was there to meet me at the airport along with a couple of charter pilots. He ended up pumping 165 litres into the fuel tanks, much more than was necessary for the relatively short 178NM hop to Port Hedland, but he wanted to make the best contribution he could. He further stunned me by telling me he had rung the refuellers in Port Hedland and Derby (my next landing points) to do likewise! After carrying out repairs to the cross-threaded long-range fuel cap and applying a smear of silicon to the top of the leaking fuel gauge, I was ready to depart for Port Hedland just on 10.00am. With an aerodrome elevation of 1,460 feet, a substantial fuel load and the temperature starting to rise, *Margery* took a considerable time to become airborne.

The landscape was rugged for most of the way with very little sign of activity on the ground anywhere. The rich red and green colours of Wittenoom Gorge in the Hamersley Range were stunning and it was hard to believe that this same place had been the centre and cause of so much pain and suffering through asbestos mining. Blue asbestos, used in building and industrial applications, was mined here in the 1950s and 60s. Asbestos tailings were a by-product of the mining process and it was the inhalation of airborne asbestos fibres from the tailings that caused the problem. Asbestos-related diseases include asbestosis, lung cancer and mesothelioma. A high percentage of the original mine workers and town inhabitants have died from these diseases, in a number of cases, some forty years later. The mine had long since closed, but remnants of the deserted mine buildings and a couple of surviving houses in the now ghost-like town were clearly visible.

At 30NM out I was given a straight-in approach for runway 36 by Port Hedland Tower. The town of Port Hedland is situated 5NM further west on the coast and is a major port for the Pilbara Region from where huge quantities of iron ore are shipped. By tonnage, it is one of the largest ports in the world. I managed a good landing in the hot, gusty conditions and was very pleased to see Carol and Campbell and his family. Two RFDS pilots and a local newspaper reporter were also there to meet me. After refuelling, Campbell drove us to the motel in town and we had a pleasant afternoon and evening together. Flight time to Port

Hedland had been just 2.6 hours, so it had been an enjoyable, low-stress day.

The next day, 29 April, we awoke around 6.00am and after a quick breakfast, drove straight to the airport. This was Day 4 of the flight and for the first three days, I had been concerned at how sluggish *Margery* was on take-off. Since Carol was about to return to Perth, it was an opportune time to off-load some baggage and I was able to eliminate about 3-4kg of weight. The items jettisoned included several electric power point adaptors for the different countries I would travel through, computer cables and jacks, transformer and a tin of perspex cleaner.

Just before leaving Port Hedland, Campbell offered me his Bible and, in order to keep the weight down, it was decided I would take just the Book of Psalms and the New Testament. Without hesitation, he ripped these sections from the Bible and handed them to me. I read passages from these every night of my trip: they gave me solace and strength. Amanda-Sue had made me a couple of rounds of sandwiches for a mid-air lunch and Carol had given me some muesli bars and cold water – the provisions would seldom be this good.

Campbell swung the propeller and with a light breeze blowing from the south, I took off at 9.00am. The tower approved one circuit and as I passed over the top, I could see the small family group waving goodbye. I felt a tinge of sadness, realising this was the last I would see of my family for … who knew how long?

The brown coastal mudflats were clearly visible as I departed Port Hedland and commenced a slow, steady climb to my planned cruising altitude of 5,500 feet. I experienced a very smooth ride for the first hour or so, followed by light turbulence for the remainder of the leg. Navigation was relatively easy as just over two thirds of the flight was coastal or near-coastal. I flew over the well known landmarks of Eighty Mile Beach, Anna Plains and Frazier Downs Stations, and La Grange Mission. I could see mangroves along the water's edge for the first time on the Western Australian coastline. *Margery's* ground speed was 65 knots to start with, which rose to 70-75 knots closer to Derby.

As I approached the airport, a strangely beautiful landscape lay before me – gently swirling colours of light brown and cream formed by the intertwining of mudflats and sandbars: it had a flat, almost satin-like appearance. The windsock indicated about 10 knots blowing straight down Runway 29, so I chose that one and executed what I thought was a good landing. It had been a fairly long flight of five-and-a-half hours. Refuelling was carried out straight away and Bill Simons, who runs the Mobil refuelling facility, refused any payment for the 130 litres pumped aboard. Once again, amazing generosity.

A local businessman, Trevor Birch (himself a pilot), had heard I was coming through and came out to the airport to meet me and take me back into town. Feeling hot and tired, I wanted to go to my motel and have a shower, but Trevor said the Derby Council had just finished their monthly meeting and would like to meet me. I was so glad I did go, for they were a lively bunch from a variety of backgrounds. One elderly councillor was an Englishman who had lived in Australia since he was thirteen, but was obviously still proud of his heritage and had retained his strong English accent. Two councillors were Aborigines and the remainder white Australians. It was an informal and happy meeting. Before finally taking me to my quarters for the night, Trevor drove me to a vantage point to see the highest tide in Derby for the year – 12 metres.

The next day, Day 5 of my trip, was my first planned rest day. I was looking forward to it as I would be able to carry out some servicing on *Margery,* as well as take care of overdue washing. I was also keen to go for a walk, for after so many inactive hours in the cockpit, I felt it was important to exercise my body to maintain a reasonable degree of fitness. I went to bed tired but happy.

I slept in until 7.30am – a luxury! When planning the trip I was uncertain as to what should be my final departure point from Australia after Derby: Kulin Island, which lay just a couple of hours to the north, or Troughton Island which was about 287NM, south-west of Darwin and 264NM north-east of Derby. The latter would add a day to my trip, but deep down I felt it was the safer option as it was slightly closer to Timor and had a better airstrip. I had prepared flight plans and arranged fuel for both islands with the idea of making my final decision in Derby.

Following breakfast I had two radio interviews – one with Ted Bull from the ABC and the other with Cecile O'Connor from GWN (Golden West Network).

At the airport I was asked by Trevor Birch's son, Jason (a commercial pilot), if I would like to join two tourists he was taking for a joy-flight over the Buccaneer Archipelago. His aircraft was a Cessna 210 and I jumped at the opportunity. This time I could relax and just soak up the scenery. The spectacle of the thousand or so islands that make up the Archipelago was magnificent with a highlight being the Horizontal Waterfalls. The waterfalls are up to 4 metres in height and are created by tidal water flowing between two gaps in parallel ridges which form part of the McLarty Ranges. They occur at both neap and ebb tides and are an unusual and picturesque sight in an ocean setting. It also just happened that this two-hour sightseeing tour took us past Kulin Island. I made up my mind, there and then, that I would not land there. It had a considerable upward slope at one end and seemed to be perched precariously on top of a ridge.

Once back at Derby Airport an oil change was carried out and I serviced both magnetos and adjusted the tappets. At around 5.20pm the engine cowls were refastened and the engine given a short run-up. It ran sweetly, and I must say I felt pleased with myself as this was the first time I had serviced the magnetos and adjusted the tappets on my own.

The Derby Council organised an informal dinner and reception for me that night and presented me with a letter addressed to Derby City Council in England, which I was to post upon my arrival – a regression to the earliest form of airmail. I excused myself at 8.20pm – I had the distinct impression they were going to party on, but was keen to get back to my room and check over my charts and flight plan for tomorrow. My daughter, April, faxed me additional information for the Derby-Troughton Island track, which was appreciated.

At the airport next morning, 1 May, I was surprised at the number of people who'd gathered to see me off, thirty school children and a similar number of adults. The local police sergeant walked up to me and, without warning, placed me in handcuffs. He told me, severely, that I was under arrest, without giving any reason, and then said to the assembled onlookers, "The only way I will release Mr Markham and allow him to continue on his way is if you pay the fine I have set at $100." To the delight of all he added, "When the $100 is paid, I order that it be forwarded direct to the Royal Flying Doctor Service." What a novel and entertaining way to raise funds! Within minutes the $100 was paid, plus more!

Once out of the handcuffs I loaded up *Margery* and prepared to depart. After lift-off I flew straight over the top of the small band of waving well-wishers and set course to cross the top end of Western Australia in a north-easterly direction. The views from above were spectacular as I traversed the rugged and beautiful landscape of Secure Bay, Walcott Inlet, Prince Regent River, Frederick Harbour and then a small group of uninhabited islands in the Admiralty Gulf region, some 35NM south-west of Troughton Island. The small, pristine, white beaches and massive, cliff-faced islands of mesa formation are sights I shall never forget.

I was nervous about landing on Troughton Island as it is small and flat and subject to strong crosswinds. Given the dimensions of the island, approximately 1,450 metres x 800 metres, the 1,040 metre gravel runway has been built down the middle in a NW/SE direction (runways 14 and 32, i.e. reciprocal compass headings of 140° and 320°), which is practically at right angles to the prevailing winds.

Since Troughton is such a small island I didn't sight it until I was 10 miles away, and at the precise moment I did, I was greeted by Blackie, the friendly island radio operator.

He advised me that the wind at ground level was around 12 knots and coming from an east, south-easterly direction, so I opted for Runway 14. This meant that the wind would be coming from my left, though I would still be generally landing into wind. I felt excited as I flew downwind of the airstrip and had a bird's eye view of this tiny coral island with no trees and just a handful of simple buildings. I made a good landing with an estimated crosswind component of around 8 knots. A few of the locals had come out to greet me. It really is a beautiful little island and I felt the relaxed, almost serene atmosphere immediately. Troughton Island is used by BHP as a base for helicopters to service their oil rigs in the Timor Sea. The maximum number of people on the island, at any one time, is around a dozen.

The locals made me feel very welcome and I enjoyed a substantial evening meal of rack of lamb, roast vegetables, apple pie and cream. I was seated with two helicopter pilots – one was Barney Williams, the Island Manager – which gave me the opportunity to find out, first hand, what I could expect for my first ocean crossing the next day. Apart from telling me that the weather would be okay and that I should track to Kupang via the 285m long *Jabiru Venture*, a converted oil tanker now used as a floating oil production facility, they seemed unperturbed about my pending, long over-water flight. This helped to allay my fears and I spent the rest of the meal feeling relaxed and discussing a wide range of subjects with them.

After dinner I went for a walk and, at the water's edge,

watched a glorious sunset. There's something calming about observing a sunset over water and I felt a sense of inner peace as the sun slipped slowly below the horizon. The atmosphere was steamy and there was a 15-knot warm easterly blowing. I retired to my small, comfortable Donga (transportable accommodation) early and went over my maps for the next day. Despite my large dinner, I polished off a pear and banana, a couple of small cakes and a mug of tea for supper!

I also had a dress rehearsal: I tried on three money belts that contained a relatively large number of US notes in small denominations which would be used mostly in SE Asia and the Middle East to pay for fuel and airport handling charges. Beneath my flying suit one belt was suspended from my neck, another in the small of my back and the last one around my stomach. I felt decidedly uncomfortable and awkward wearing this paraphernalia and felt certain that when I landed in Kupang in West Timor tomorrow, the word GUILTY would be clearly visible in big, bold letters across my forehead. I was probably over-reacting. Yes, I had exceeded the permitted limit of US dollars, but not to any significant degree. The need to conceal the money centred more on being a potential target for muggers in South-East Asia and the Middle East, even though I had not been given any formal warning on the likelihood of such an event occurring. But apart from anything else, the US dollars were precious as I had been told by several transcontinental pilots prior to leaving Australia that it was the only form of payment that would be accepted by refuellers and ground handlers in South-East Asia and the Middle East.

# Chapter 3

# TROUGHTON ISLAND TO JAKARTA

**Days 7–10** - 2 May 1998 to 5 May 1998

O n the morning of 2 May, I inspected *Margery* prior to take-off and found the right hand tyre was partially deflated. It appeared to be only a leaking valve, but I couldn't take any chances and Dave, the island engineer, removed the tube and checked it for punctures. None were found.

I finally took off at 10.30am, a fraction nervous about crossing the Timor Sea. But, after a 20-minute climb, I reached my cruising altitude of 4,500 feet and my nerves disappeared. For most of the journey I was on top of a layer of scattered stratocumulus and it was a generally smooth run. Approximately half way across the Timor Sea I sighted the *Jabiru Venture*, an oil drilling ship, plus two smaller support vessels and circled once over the top of them.

Cookie, the chef on Troughton Island, had given me a snack to have en route, and from the size of the foil-wrapped parcel on my lap I knew it was going to be a pretty substantial snack! Eating in a Tiger Moth while flying is an awkward and hazardous operation, and even more so when you have a couple of two-inch-thick meat and tomato sauce sandwiches to contend with. The sauce ended up over a good portion of my face and running down the sleeve of my jacket and onto my flying suit. After several large hurried bites, I decided it was time to get things back under control and had no alternative but to eject the remains of the well-intentioned snack to the waiting sharks beneath me. I was in too much of a mess to consider saving it for later. I half turned *Margery* around in an attempt to see the missile going down, but it had disappeared in a flash.

There was a lot of smoke and haze surrounding Timor when I initially sighted the island some 30NM out. My next concern was my making first-ever contact with a foreign air-traffic controller. Would I be able to understand him, or her, and vice versa? I finally made contact with El Tari tower at 20NM and, to my relief, could understand the controller quite well. As I turned onto finals, *Margery* was starting to buck in the hot gusty conditions and, under the circumstances, I was quite pleased with my landing. This leg had taken just 3.2 hours, thanks to an excellent ground speed that varied between 85 knots and 104 knots.

On leaving the runway, I was instructed to taxi behind the "Follow Me" car to my parking position. After shutting down and climbing out of the cockpit I immediately donned my captain's hat (an old Ansett Airlines model without the badge) and fitted the 4-bar epaulettes to each shoulder. I'd been advised that this universally recognisable captain's ranking would gain me instant respect and ensure an easier time in dealing with airport officials and government bureaucrats. Although it seemed to work, I didn't feel comfortable at all in this bogus uniform and stopped wearing it once I reached Pakistan. I preferred to be just me, even if it did, perhaps, result in experiencing slightly less generous and courteous treatment. I handed out the first of my gold kangaroo pins to the small group who had gathered around and they seemed to be delighted to receive them.

I decided to refuel *Margery* straightaway and after only about ten minutes on the ground started to notice the tropical heat; it was certainly hotter than Troughton Island or Derby. I felt dehydrated and generally exhausted. Because of the strong wind of around 20 knots, I asked if *Margery* could be hangared and at the end of some mild bartering, taxied over to an Indonesian Air Force hangar.

The drive to the Kristal Hotel in Kupang took twenty minutes, winding through a maze of rough dirt roads before reaching a main road. Hundreds of small motorbikes were coming and going – some laden with fresh produce held in position by ingeniously constructed timber crates that were almost as big as the motorbike. Yet others carried Mum and Dad with a small child sandwiched in between them on the seat and, occasionally, a second child standing on the footplate between their father's knees while holding onto the handlebars. The constant honking of motorbike and car horns was incredible as riders and drivers made their presence felt in order to force their way to their destination. If one views an ant colony from above, everything seems chaotic, but to the ants on the ground it is a system they are used to and obviously thrive upon.

The streets of Kupang were also very crowded and there were hundreds of small wayside shops and stalls and a large number of unfinished new buildings. Perhaps they had run out of funds? Being in a totally foreign country for the first time on my trip, and having just left the vast and relatively unpopulated state of Western Australia, I found this confronting to the senses and something of a culture shock.

Later in the day I rang Carol and we had a good chat about home and how everyone was getting on. She encouraged me to go and join a group of Australian Navy sailors who were on leave from their ship and enjoying themselves in the pool area. I gave it a try, but when I found the main form of entertainment was an inflated condom being hit to one another as a kind of aerial ping-pong, I decided to retire to my room – not quite my idea of fun! Back in my room, ABC Radio in Adelaide rang for an on-air interview and Carol was also linked up to listen in.

I had decided if the winds were favourable in the morning I would try and bypass Waingapu, a planned stop, and head straight for Bali. I would pick up a day this way. Crossing the Timor Sea had boosted my confidence and I noted in my diary:

*Feel that I have achieved a small milestone today and going to bed happy.*

My watch alarm went off at 5.30am on the morning of 3 May. I'd had a reasonable night's sleep, despite my Aussie neighbours who hadn't gone to bed and were still making a racket at around 4.00am. I didn't really mind though and headed straight to the airport to do the usual paper work.

I took off just after 8.00am, and before long, was recording a ground speed of 100-104 knots – just what I wanted as it meant that I could overfly Waingapu and continue on to Bali, 308NM to the west. However, when I went to retrieve the map for the Waingapu-Bali leg I could not find it in the cockpit, so had no alternative but to land. I put *Margery* down in a very strong, hot and gusty crosswind. Waingapu Airport is situated near the northern coast of Sumba Island and 2NM miles south-east of the townsite. When calling inbound to Waingapu, I did not feel any need to tell them about my plan to retrieve the Bali map and thought it would be a simple matter of landing, grabbing the map and taking off again – all in the space of about ten minutes. Although the airport had the typical Indonesian red and white check control tower, there wasn't a soul to be seen anywhere and *Margery* was the only aircraft in sight. As planned, I quickly went to retrieve the required map from the baggage compartment, but, to my great annoyance, found that it was in the cockpit after all and there had been no need to land. I prepared to make a hasty departure as I didn't want to be delayed any further, but just as I was about to swing the propeller I spotted a man striding quickly towards me. He was neatly dressed, spoke perfect English and it was soon apparent he was the air traffic controller.

We had a rather spirited but polite discussion. I was adamant about what I was doing, explaining that Waingapu was not a scheduled stop, that I had only landed to retrieve a map from the baggage compartment and that I was departing for Bali immediately. He was equally adamant that I wasn't going anywhere until I had spoken to his boss. My reluctance to comply with his wish resulted in his taking hold of my wrist and leading me to the boss's house, which was about 200 metres away through a section of jungle on the perimeter of the airfield. Since I was on my own in an isolated location, I resisted the strong urge to wrench my arm from his grip. I believe I managed to appear calm and unperturbed, but inwardly I was seething.

I waited on the verandah of a neatly kept cottage whilst my escort summoned his boss. After a minute or two he came out onto the verandah and sat down on a chair whilst my escort and I remained standing. He was a short man of medium build and around forty years of age. Although his clothes were ordinary and not very clean, he possessed the air of someone in authority and spoke a reasonable standard of English. I thought he might have been a government official, though he didn't ask to see any papers.

We were in a relatively secluded area and, apart from the three of us, I did not see another person. For this reason, and not knowing what his intentions were, I felt slightly apprehensive. He quizzed me for about ten minutes with such questions as "Where have you come from?" "What is your next destination?" "What is your fuel capacity and how much is in your tanks?" It became clear to me that his only real interest was to try and sell me fuel. *Perhaps he ran the refuelling business?* I thought. After finally convincing him that I had more than sufficient fuel to reach Bali, I was allowed to leave. Transiting aircraft were obviously few and far between in these parts.

We returned via the control tower to fill out a form or two and I was astonished at what a primitive set-up it was with the controller, my escort, the only one on duty. It was apparent that the bottom section of the tower doubled as accommodation for his family.

The wind was now extremely strong and gusty and jungle palms bordering the left side of the runway were bending and swaying wildly. I just managed to keep *Margery* on the runway with full left aileron and sufficient forward stick to balance her on the main wheels waiting for lift-off. As soon as lift-off was achieved I kicked the nose into wind and crabbed out of the airfield to my assigned altitude. I was relieved to get away for more reasons than one. The cloud was now steadily building up over Waingapu, or to describe it in more technical terms – stratocumulus, 2,000 feet AGL (above ground level) to 7,000 feet plus.

Once over the ocean, the air smoothed out again and I soon achieved a ground speed of between 90 and 100 knots. Initially, my course took me well south of Sumbawa Island and then to hug the southern coast of Lombok Island. I seemed to be over water forever that day and of the 5.8 hours total, just 1 was over land. When 80NM from Bali I called up on frequency 121.5 and was pleased when Qantas 31 answered and said they would pass on my position and ETA to Bali Control. I finally made contact with Bali Control when 50NM out.

The scenery on approaching Bali was beautiful, particularly Mt Agung majestically poking through clouds in the distance, its peak 10,309 feet above sea level. When about 3NM from the runway I asked the Air Traffic Controller the wind speed and direction and he replied that it was only 5 knots and about 30° off the nose for the runway heading. On finals he told me it was 5 knots up to 11 knots, but it was more like 18 knots and very gusty and I had to use every ounce of concentration to pin the main wheels on the ground and bring *Margery* safely to a stop. The wind was now even stronger and although I requested temporary hangarage, none was available and I spent considerable time securing *Margery* to a grassed area at one end of the airport.

Prior to leaving the airport I wanted to finalise the airport charges and I asked the ground handling agent what the fee was. After a moment's thought he said, "$500 US". I told him that in Kupang I had only been charged US$200 so why the big difference? Without hesitation he responded – "Okay $225 US". Obviously he was trying it on. Around US$225 to US$250 became the standard fee throughout South-East Asia, until I reached the middle-east where it quadrupled.

By now I was feeling extremely hot and tired. It had been a long, eventful day and I couldn't wait to get out of my gear. I took a taxi to the Bintang Bali, one of the premier hotels of Bali where I was staying courtesy of Malaysia Airlines. I soaked for ages in a deep, warm bath and after a wholesome dinner of leek soup, pork and rice I had fully recovered. I rang Carol and then Bradley, whose wife Marie was expecting a baby any day. These brief contacts with home meant a lot to me and strengthened my resolve.

A note in my diary reads:

> *Might have pulled a muscle in my chest propping the Tiger today – sternum quite sore.*

But as I discovered during the rest of the trip, aches and pains, with one exception, were short-lived. More serious matters were bad weather, being low on fuel and feeling the extremes of heat and cold.

The following morning, 4 May, I was up at 5.00am and ready for the short run to Surabaya on Java – about 2½ hours flying.

Within minutes of departure my transponder failed, despite several attempts to recycle it. The air traffic controller told me to steer 274° and climb to 4,500 feet, but I soon found myself in light cloud and had to descend to 1,000 feet to remain visual. When pushing the face of the transponder I found it was totally loose in its cradle. Fortunately, I had an allen key in the side pocket of the cockpit and managed to screw it in tight. It worked well after that. An hour later I entered the Bali Strait which separates the islands of Bali and Java. I passed between two mountain peaks 15NM apart on the north-east tip of Java, Mt Merapi and Ljen Crater standing at 9,186 feet on my left and Mt Baluran, 4,183 feet, on my right. The lush green landscape incorporating these and several other mountain peaks was spectacular. The final hour of this leg was over the Madura Strait travelling just north of the tiny, picturesque Kepalang Island. About half-an-hour out of Surabaya, on the north coast of Java, I flew over hundreds of acres of fish ponds which abutted the coast line and came well out into the Strait.

As I flew closer to Surabaya, visibility deteriorated badly and I had difficulty in seeing Juanda Airport until just a few nautical miles away. The cloud base just north of the airport was 1,000 feet or less. For the final ten minutes of the flight, the air traffic controller directed me to change my course (called radar-vectoring) to allow a couple of commercial flights to land.

After tying *Margery* down for the night, I called for a taxi and was taken on a long drive to my hotel.

This was the ninth day of the journey and I was beginning to feel the effects of being confined for hours on end in the tight Tiger Moth cockpit, so I spent an hour in the Olympic Gymnasium that formed part of the hotel complex. I concluded the workout with a sauna and felt a lot better for it. I rang home and asked April to try and source some weather information for me for tomorrow as obtaining reliable weather information in Surabaya seemed to be impossible.

I did another radio interview with Ron Tate from the ABC in Perth and in the evening had a pleasant dinner with Simon Johnson, the director of the Western Australian Trade Office in Indonesia, and his family.

My final diary note for the day read:

> *My spirit is good; feel a bit tired at the end of each day's flight, but recover well overnight – I hope that's the pattern for the rest of the trip.*

I was up at 5.00am on 5 May and, after a light breakfast, headed straight for the airport. Once again it was a long trip through heavy traffic, hundreds of weaving motorbikes and plenty of horn honking. What amazed me in this traffic nightmare was that there was no visible road rage, as you would find back in Australia!

I lodged my flight plan, refuelled and took off at 9.10am local time. The cloud base was low, around 1,500-1,800 feet, and after the first twenty minutes, I thought about turning back. But, according to the weather reports from April and the airport, it should start to improve as I moved westwards. So I continued on and after about an hour it did improve and remained so for the next one-and-a-half hours. The final two hours, though, were quite bad – decreasing visibility with a lot of haze and low cloud, with one large patch of cloud down to the ground. This two hour stretch was approximately between Brebes near the northern Java coast and Jakarta, and just left of my course was a considerable mountain range with the highest visible peak being Mt Tjareme at 10,098 feet. In clearer weather I should imagine the landscape would be stunning. I first made contact with Halim Airport some 30NM out, but on account of the bad haze, didn't sight the airport until just 3NM away.

A number of airport ground crew and officials came out to greet me and I couldn't wait to tell them about the bird-strike I'd experienced in the early part of the leg. An hour into the flight, as I was approaching my first waypoint of Odjanegoro, I sighted a blurred object just forward and above that thumped me hard on the head before disappearing. If nothing else, it shocked me into a state of high alertness and if I hadn't been concentrating a hundred percent before then, I certainly was now.

I indicated the approximate size of the bird to the assembled group and there followed an intense discussion as to what type of bird it was, even down to its colouring. Then when I climbed on top of the engine cowl to remove the fuel cap, located between two upper wings, I found it was missing. That's what had hit me on the head! How embarrassing! It would have been stretching things a bit too far to have suggested to those present that I had experienced two incidents en route – a bird strike and a lost fuel cap. The airport staff were very helpful and tried every type of cap they could get their hands on, including the cap of a 44-gallon drum, but nothing would fit.

It was getting late in the day and I asked someone to take me to a machine shop. I had now been at the airport for several hours and was feeling extremely hot. My flying suit was saturated with perspiration, as was the paper money in the money belts beneath the suit. After some twenty minutes driving through crowded, narrow back streets we came to a workshop and to my great delight, I could see a line of lathes. I drew a sketch from memory and they said they could manufacture one for me in brass and that it would cost 50,000 rupiah or about A$30. A machinist drove back with us to the airport with a small thread measuring device and to measure the precise diameter of the opening to the tank. They said it would be ready for me by morning and I couldn't believe how kind and obliging they were.

Jakarta, the capital of Indonesia, is a sprawling, bustling city of around ten million people. Once again, small motorcycles abound and appear to be the main form of transport. The traffic is chaotic and pollution levels are high. Modern, multi-storey office blocks, apartments and hotels within the city precinct stand out and are in distinct contrast to older, poorer class buildings and shacks such as the one where the fuel cap was made.

After sharing tea and cake with several of the airport ground handlers in their tiny office, I lodged my flight plan and finally arrived at the Shangrila Hotel at 6.30pm, exhausted. I phoned home and spoke to Carol, April and Alison and was happy to hear that baby Bonnie was born to Brad and Marie today – our third grandchild!

On checking my clothes, I realised I had left a bundle of washing in Surabaya, but I still had enough to get by with.

The Shangrila was the plushest hotel I had stayed in so far, once again, courtesy of Malaysia Airlines. Everything was electronically operated including the curtains, and the bed was huge – three pillows across. Unfortunately, I would barely have time to enjoy this luxury, for I would be up before dawn.

# Chapter 4

# JAKARTA TO SINGAPORE

**Days 11-15** - 6 May 1998 to 10 May 1998

After fitting the new fuel cap I was ready for departure. It was Day 11 of the journey, 6 May. When I left Jakarta's Halim Airport the conditions weren't particularly good, though from the weather report I obtained it looked as though it might improve. To begin with, Halim approach directed me a considerable distance off-track, around Hatta (the major airport) and visibility was very poor. They then put me on a heading of 300°, told me to maintain an altitude of 3,500 feet and basically left me to it.

After flying for about forty-five minutes I picked up the distinctive outline of Banten Bay followed by Pandjang Island and then Padjut Point, the northern tip of Java. I determined I was about 12NM south-west of my planned track and decided that I would rejoin this track at Maringgai, on the island of Sumatra, some 40NM to the north west. With the exception of a few miles, this revised section of my track would all be over open water.

As I flew over the Sunda Strait, which separates the islands of Java and Sumatra, storm clouds were steadily building up and both sea and sky were an eerie, grey colour. I was hoping the weather would improve once over the Sumatran mainland, but on reaching the coast, it hadn't. I decided to continue on at least until Maringgai, a few miles inland, and reassess the situation. Once I reached the small settlement of Maringgai the weather deteriorated suddenly. I obeyed the golden rule of doing a 180° turn in such a situation to return to my departure point, in this case Jakarta.

But on completing the turn I was horrified to see a dark mass of cloud right in front of me and with no way around it. So I immediately turned back onto my original course, believing that the only way out of this mess was to push on towards Palembang. For the first few seconds of this confrontation with nature, my heart picked up a beat or two and I felt an adrenalin rush. "This is what the trip is all about," I said to myself, "this is the adventure I have secretly craved for so long."

But this sense of bravado and the wry smile on my face quickly disappeared when I realised the seriousness of the situation. Rain was bucketing down and my flying jacket and the folded map on my knee were becoming soaked. To make things worse I was down to 2,000 feet from my previous cruising altitude of 4,000 feet, and the cloud base immediately above me descended to tree-top height just a few miles ahead. I had no option but to follow the cloud base down until I was now, at the most, just 300 feet above the jungle canopy with a forward visibility of less than 1 kilometre. The only comfort I had was the steady, rhythmic beat of *Margery's* Gipsy engine up front and I was pinning every hope on her that she would get me through. The palm trees and thatched roofed cottages that passed beneath me were now alarmingly clear as I looked for an escape route. I even prayed. I dared not go any lower for fear of hitting an uncharted object and, although I couldn't see them, from my map I was very much aware that there were three hills which exceeded 800 feet to the left of my track. Mirah Mountain, with a height of 820 feet was just 3NM left of track and totally unsighted. For this reason I deliberately altered my heading 5° to the right. After holding on for what seemed an eternity, I could see the cloud ahead was starting to thin and slowly, but surely, I climbed back up to 4,000 feet. I had noted the time of entering the storm as 5.24 UTC and coming out of it as 5.47 UTC: a twenty-three minute episode in my life I shall never forget. But things got worse.

As I continued on towards Palembang, the ground below was glistening from the torrential rain that had fallen and the landscape had the appearance of a giant swamp for as far as the eye could see. I made contact with Palembang Tower at twenty miles and was told to call again at five miles, but to my horror, I could see another massive storm of about 10NM radius appearing to totally blanket the airport and surrounds ahead of me. The tower controller obviously couldn't appreciate the serious threat this weather was imposing from my position and was telling me to come in. When I did make an attempt, the cloud base was less than 500 feet and poor *Margery* received a severe shaking for daring to go so close. Given my torrid experience of barely an hour ago, I told the controller I was going to hold 10NM west of Palembang until it cleared.

I went into my own impromptu holding pattern over water-logged farm lands for at least forty minutes, and still it wasn't clearing. With impenetrable masses of black cloud separating me from Palembang and now slowly moving towards me, I had to quickly start thinking of my remaining options. Fuel wasn't a problem as I estimated I still had three hours remaining, but where could I land? And then in the distance, to the north, I spotted some clear sky. I immediately headed in that direction, maintaining 1,000 feet. I surmised that if the storm was moving westwards and I could get around the top of it, then I might be able to enter Palembang from the back of the storm as it passed through. By this time, the tower controller was not responding to my calls requesting details of present visibility at the airfield and whether or not it was improving, so I was left feeling lonely and worried. Then, without warning, a Merpati Airline captain, who had just departed Palembang and had obviously heard my calls, told me that the storm had passed and visibility was 10NM.

It was a huge relief to have the airfield in sight. I was pleased with my landing. Palembang is a pretty little airfield with friendly ground staff. It was satisfying to see their eyes light up when I handed out more gold kangaroo pins. I refuelled, lodged my flight plan for the next day and checked at the Met. office to see how the weather was shaping up.

The taxi drive to the hotel took about twenty-five minutes and the town centre seemed quite poor with no modern buildings. On account of the heavy rain, there were large pools of muddy water on the sides of the roads. I was somewhat shocked to see the tiny figure of a naked child, barely four years of age, bend down and scoop up a handful of this water to drink. I immediately thought of the risk of disease to this poor mite, but in an instant our taxi had passed and we were continuing on our way to the hotel and passing further images of poverty. It is a sight that still haunts me; I wonder where that child is now and hope that life has been kind.

With an estimated population of 1,400,000, Palembang is the largest city on the island of Sumatra, as well as being a deepwater port on the River Musi which caters for ocean going vessels. The Grand Mosque, built in 1740, is a prominent city landmark.

On arrival at the hotel, I had a shower and then rang home. I always felt a lot better once I was out of my hot, sweaty flying suit. I had soup and satay sticks for dinner which went down well.

My diary note for the day started with:

*Well, I know that God was with me today: some of the most trying conditions I have ever encountered .... It's been a very difficult day and I'm certainly not taking off tomorrow if the weather is marginal – but really want to get to Singapore .... Paint was stripped from part of right aileron and a small nick on the propeller – all happened today – probably severity of rain.*

The next morning, 7 May, I was up at 5.30am, full of hope that I would reach Singapore. I even skipped breakfast to save time: a couple of muesli bars during the flight would do. The ground handling agent picked me up in his car and drove me to the immigration officer's house to have my passport stamped for exiting Indonesia. And then it was on to the airport. After visiting the Met. Office, where I was told the weather looked good and was getting even better, I confirmed my flight plan and took off at 7.20am local time.

Flying over the Beerhala Strait, almost halfway to Singapore, I noticed a huge wall of cloud ahead stretching from sea level to 10,000 feet and more, and left and right as far as the eye could see. For forty minutes I attempted to find a passage through it, but to no avail. I eventually decided it was a definite no-go and headed back to Palembang with great reluctance. The cloud was now starting to build up on the return journey and I hoped that it would hold sufficiently for me to get back safely. It was stratocumulus with a base of around 2,000 feet, so I flew most of the way on top.

When I landed at Palembang, I had been airborne for four hours and was feeling hot, tired and disappointed. Following refuelling, the Airport Controller approached me and, aware of the bad weather I had encountered and at the sight of my small and seemingly fragile Tiger Moth, aired his concern for my safety.

He also admitted that the weather forecast I had been given wasn't adequate and I appreciated his honesty.

It rained heavily during the afternoon and from my hotel window I could see the street below was awash. The power also went off about half a dozen times and I was glad to be safe and secure in my temporary lodgings.

Ever hopeful, I was up at 5.00am the following morning and once more visited the immigration officer's house to have the exit date amended in my passport. Approaching the airport, I could see a big build-up of cloud to the north already, and deep down I knew it was a no-go situation again. The official meteorological report only confirmed my beliefs. A statement at the top of the report could not have been clearer: "Seasonal monsoon flow continues to dominate weather throughout the forecast region." The diagram included in the report showed a massive cloud build-up covering the whole of Borneo and stretching across to the Singapore/Palembang regions. A phone call to the Singapore Meteorological Office confirmed that this whole weather system was slowly moving eastward, but it might take a day or two to clear.

Poor *Margery* had been left out in very heavy rain over the past twenty-four hours, and as more was on the way, I decided to try and find a hangar for the night. The only one available was at the other end of the field, about a kilometre away and, fortunately, I was given permission to use it. Once in the hangar I carried out water drain checks, including removing the fuel drain bowl and re-lock wiring it (there were only two drops of water). I also replaced gaffer tape on the right aileron, a temporary repair of two days before, as it was puffed up and distorted with water.

Back at the hotel, I related my frustrations to Ali, a young university student who was working at the hotel part-time. He asked if I'd like to see his university and also have a tour of Palembang with his friends, Ahmad, and a young woman, Nur.

We ended up sharing lunch together at Nur's parents' home and I spent a delightful and interesting three hours with them.

Later I rang home and it was so heartening to hear familiar voices again. John Roberts from Perth, who had assisted with my initial planning for the trip, came up with detailed weather information from the US Navy Weather Service and the indications were that tomorrow was not going to be any better.

I had a solid forty-minute workout in a gymnasium adjoining the hotel, which helped to get rid of the pent up frustration I was feeling at not being able to move on. I comment in my diary:

> *As I write, I can hear cars sloshing through the rain-soaked roads outside. Although I badly want to reach Singapore, there is something about the sound of rain I find quite comforting. Thunder outside also – glad Margery is away. I think the forced rest in Palembang has done me some good and to make up time, may forgo the planned rest day in Singapore.*

Saturday, 9 May, was yet another wasted day in Palembang as a result of an early morning telephone conversation with a Singapore weather forecaster who advised, "Embedded CB's (cumulonimbus-thunderstorms) between Palembang and Singapore – getting better over the next couple of days – big systems – not very suitable for small aircraft."

Apart from a radio interview with the BBC in London, I spent the day quietly going over maps and flight plans for the next few stages, reading and watching CNN on television. I also spoke with Carol and brother Roger, and his wife Dianne, back home – they gave me a lift.

Late in the afternoon, I heard the loud wailing of sirens and saw on the street below three police trucks and armoured vehicles, including one which had a water cannon mounted on top. They were on their way to quell yet another student riot or demonstration.

The television news report showed that the situation had been much worse in Jog Jakarta (Java) with the burning of cars and motorbikes – particularly those owned by the Chinese. The apparent cause of the riots was the Indonesian Government raising charges for various items and most significantly, petrol.

The next morning I was up at 4.45am and determined to get to Singapore no matter what – well, within reason. It was Mother's Day, 10 May, and I reflected for a moment on my own wonderful mother and also that I would be flying in her namesake on this day. To save time, and because it was so early, I skipped breakfast again and headed for the airport, and once more obtained immigration clearance on the way.

Departing at precisely 7.20am there was only 3km visibility at Palembang, but I managed to climb to 4,500 feet on top of a layer of scattered stratocumulus cloud. Through gaps in the cloud, I could clearly see the broad and muddy Banjuasin River pass beneath me and was reminded of the Silkair Boeing 737 that went down in the Musi River, not far from here, just five months earlier. The circumstances were mysterious and it was alleged the pilot, Captain Tsu Way Ming, may have committed suicide, with a total of 104 lives being lost.

Crossing Benawang Bay, I headed out over the sea, tracking for my next reporting point, Singkep Airport on Singkep Island. For the moment, flying on top of this carpet of white cloud, everything seemed serene, but up ahead and to my right, towering peaks of cumulonimbus were already forming and I was beginning to feel uneasy.

I was now abeam Djablang Point on the island of Sumatra and was confronted with the almost identical position of three days ago: another massive wall of cloud, but perhaps not as dense this time. I had been in the air for two hours in reasonably good conditions, but things were about to change dramatically.

Because of the cloud base, I descended to 1,200 feet and

was now about 30NM from Singkep. The weather was still deteriorating, but I reasoned I should be able to safely make Singkep and once there, reassess my options. Singkep was reasonably clear when I arrived over the top of the airfield, so I decided to make for Singapore. Managing to climb back up to 4,500 feet, I was now between two layers of cloud and the space between them was gradually diminishing. Singapore Radar hadn't responded to my calls and I was relieved when a Singapore Airlines Captain (Flight 135) called me saying he had heard my unanswered transmission and would relay a message for me. Singapore Radar finally did make contact and for the next half hour vectored me around a number of thunderstorm cells. But the weather deteriorated even further and I had to descend rather rapidly to 3,000 feet, 2,500 feet and then 1,500 feet. With still further deterioration, I levelled out just 500 feet above the sea, with a forward visibility of only a couple of kilometres and basically no horizon. As I had experienced on the Jakarta-Palembang leg, the ocean and the sky had melted into one and taken on a sinister, greyish-brown colour. I could sense the electricity in the relatively still, warm air. If ever I felt alone and helpless in my life, this was it.

A mixed feeling of desperation and fear, and perhaps even panic, welled up in me, and it took a conscious effort to suppress it, for I knew the only one who could extract me from this predicament was me, and God willing, I would make it. And yes, I once again prayed. It was a frightening, stressful situation and didn't let up. I was now way off course and flying by the seat of my pants just to survive. I still endeavoured to fly *Margery* as accurately as I could, maintaining wings level, turn and bank indicator centred, RPM not above 2,100 and maintaining my own assigned altitude as best I could. My heading was constantly changing as I tried to avoid cloud, but I continued on in the general direction of Singapore. It was a far more serious situation than I had experienced on the Jakarta-Palembang leg five days earlier. Being low over the sea with virtually no horizon is a most dangerous situation at any time.

Then, straining my eyes, I could just make out the faint outline of two islands in the distance which immediately gave me a physical reference for straight and level flight. I dared not take my eyes off them. After a while, I re-established contact with Singapore Radar and stressed the importance of remaining in contact with them so that I could receive radar vectoring. Eventually, I managed to gain more height which in turn improved radio reception. This episode had been going on for over an hour and from the time I first encountered the wall of cloud 30NM south of Singkep, I had been flying in trying conditions for over two hours.

I've never seen an airstrip look so good than when I sighted Seletar in Singapore. On vacating the runway, I noticed a rather tall chap walking up the taxiway to greet me. It was Ray Vuillerman, a Singapore Airlines 747 captain who is also a Tiger Moth enthusiast. He made me feel most welcome and after refuelling, drove me to my hotel for the night. I was also fortunate to have hangarage for *Margery*. Just after landing, the Tower had asked me to see the supervisor of Singapore Approach. We had a friendly chat and he obviously understood the difficulties I had experienced that day.

Once at the hotel, I ran a deep bath and just soaked in it, reflecting upon the day. My diary entry read:

> *Looking forward to bed tonight and I can once again say*
> *that my prayers were answered in a real hour of need.*

After a poor night's sleep, probably because of the stressful flight I had experienced, I was up at 5.00am and keen to push on to Penang. At the airport, I obtained a weather report and lodged my flight plan. While waiting for the plan to be approved, I had the compulsory talk with the Air Traffic Controller. The reason for this is that Seletar Airport is very close to the Malaysian border and also the Sultan of Johore's estate. It follows that there are very strict rules on departing Seletar and avoiding, in particular, the Sultan's property. My flight plan was then rejected by Johore ATC and I waited until 4.00pm for them to come up with a revised plan. I had my rest day in Singapore after all!

Throughout the day I reflected on how far I had come – just over a quarter of the way – the weather problems I had experienced and how far there was still to go. They were slightly negative feelings. I soon countered them though with thoughts of the tremendous support I was receiving from family and friends back home and how I couldn't let them down, let alone myself. I also learnt a lesson from this: not to look too far ahead, but instead, to concentrate on the day in hand. I likened this to commencing a long run up a steep hill. If you keep looking to the top of the hill it is daunting and dampens your spirits and saps your energy. But if you keep looking at the ground in front of you, you will eventually get there, one step at a time.

A couple of minor repairs were carried out on *Margery* during the day: fixing a broken hinge on the engine baffle plate and a broken bracket that holds a small securing pin for the baffle plate rod. I also realised that I didn't have reading glasses anymore – just something else I had lost along the way and, for some reason, most of it had been clothing. The loss of the glasses didn't affect my map-reading when flying though, as I'd had corrective lenses glued into the lower sections of my flying goggles. Items of clothing lost included two shirts and several underpants and pairs of socks: only a couple of each item were left when I arrived in England!

# Chapter 5

# SINGAPORE TO RANGOON

**Days 16-22** - 11 May 1998 to 17 May 1998

The following morning, 11 May, I was awoken at 5.00am sharp by the now familiar beep-beep-beep of my watch alarm; no breakfast and straight to the airport by 6.10am. After showing my passport to Immigration, I pulled *Margery* from her snug resting place for the last two nights and prepared her for the flight to Penang. It was already hazy with a cloud base of around 2,500 feet and some cloud patches sitting right on the ground.

A final warning from the Briefing Office not to overfly the Sultan's Estate and within a space of ten minutes or so, I was airborne. I quickly tried to gain my bearings, but it became something of a nightmare trying to work out where I should be. It certainly wasn't as straight forward as it had seemed at the briefing. The Approach Controller also had a faulty transmitter, which made it worse, but to his credit managed to direct me away from the Sultan's Palace, just in time. A few terse words were then exchanged with the Johore Air Traffic Controller, but he managed to finish with a friendly "G'Day Mate", realising I was from Australia and that the two of us were now greatly relieved that I was away from the Sultan's sacrosanct, restricted area. What a start to this leg!

Now clear of this problem and approaching the Straits of Malacca, which separate the island of Sumatra from the Malay Peninsula, I could settle down into my flight.

For the first two hours or so, the views were not very interesting as it was overcast and there was considerable haze around. I made contact with Penang Tower at 40NM and was told to hold over a small island about 6-7NM east of Penang while the traffic cleared. The runway, which ran in a north-east, south-west direction, was just visible from this position and I could even make out a couple of commercial aircraft making their final approaches to land. This was comforting, to a degree, as I could see which runway I would be using and work out my approach. After about ten minutes, I received permission to proceed to the airport. From the air, the dark green and rugged mountain hinterland of the island of Penang clearly stood out, and in the foreground I could see a broad flat coastal strip with the airport on the south-eastern end of the island and the capital city of Georgetown visible on the north-eastern end of the island.

I was surprised to see TV cameras, press reporters and representatives of one of my sponsors, Malaysia Airline Services (MAS), waiting for my arrival, and they made quite a fuss of me. Events like this are apparently very few and far between in Penang and they certainly entered into the spirit of the occasion.

I was given a further welcome at the hotel and the MAS personnel even convened a press conference, which lasted about forty-five minutes, and then offered tea, coffee and Malay cakes. A further radio interview was conducted with Ron Tate from ABC Radio in Perth, and prior to retiring for the night, I rang home to let them know that I was safe and well and to see how they were getting along.

Lying in bed with the lights out and eyes wide open, I reflected upon the events of the day and felt peaceful: what a contrast to the wild thunderstorm and heavy rain I could hear outside! Being parked in the open, poor *Margery* was bearing the full brunt of the elements again and I just hoped that she would be all right. I would need to carry out careful water checks in the morning for possible fuel contamination.

Next day, 12 May, I was up at 5.00am and after breakfasting on a banana, muesli bar and cup of tea, headed straight to the airport. Immigration and Customs clearances were very quick and my next task was to sort out the weather. It wasn't looking particularly good but the head Met. man assured me it would improve the further north I flew. I then went to the Control Tower to lodge my flight plan. Sri, an Indian, was the controller in charge. Although he remained professional in his manner, there seemed to be a warmer side to him. I felt he empathised with the task I had in hand. Not that he said much, it was just that the thoughtful manner in which he offered advice seemed to have an element of care about it.

I departed runway 09 for Phuket in Thailand via Butterworth Air Base. There was some cloud build-up and no horizon on account of the haze. My cruising altitude for this leg was 4,500 feet, which I managed to maintain to around the halfway mark, but from then on, the cloud started to thicken and I had to descend to 1,500 feet.

Today's flight was entirely over water – the Andaman Sea. As I drew closer to Phuket Island I was surrounded by rain storms, which caused me some concern for a while. I was fascinated by showers of rain cascading from these clouds – they had the appearance of soft grey curtains connecting the clouds with the sea. But as pretty as they looked, I needed to avoid them as best I could and had to make several heading adjustments. I still couldn't see the island and because of my low altitude, wasn't able to pick up Phuket radar or tower frequencies until 30NM out. There was low cloud over Phuket when I approached and I was relieved to finally sight the runway.

I tied *Margery* down well with concrete blocks as I'd been told it could be very windy here and then had my flight plan for tomorrow's flight to Bangkok confirmed at the Briefing Office. By this time, I was very hot and sweaty and just wanted to get to my hotel for the night. But getting there in an airport limo was hellish – the young Thai driver obviously thought he was driving a Formula One car. After several near misses and the whole thirty minute drive all at 100-105km per hour, I preferred my chances in the air than with this guy on land!

I was staying at the Club Andaman Resort, courtesy of Malaysia Airlines. On arriving I was surprised to see a large welcome sign strung up at the entrance. Then a lei was placed around my neck and I was given an ice cold drink and a cold towel. It was a warm and friendly welcome.

At five in the evening, I strolled down to the beach in front of the resort. The atmosphere was balmy with a gentle breeze blowing and the ocean calm. It was also peaceful, as only a small number of people now remained and empty timber sun lounges lay in neat lines and umbrellas were folded. I walked across the white sands imprinted with thousands of footsteps and stood awhile on the shoreline listening to the sporadic lapping of small waves breaking. In front of me lay a beautiful sight; a cruise ship anchored off shore and the reflection of the sun on the water as it was beginning to set. I was on my own but not lonely. The pressures of the day had passed and the sense of peace I experienced was wonderful.

I dined on soup, steak and vegetables – my only real meal of the day – and I felt a lot better for it.

I telephoned my daughter April and sister June back in Perth and was brought up-to-date with what was happening on the home front. A member of my support team back in Perth, John Roberts, then rang through with some weather information for which I was grateful. I was also looking forward to talking to Carol, who was now in New York, en route to England.

My final task for the day was to check over the flight plan and maps for the next long leg to Bangkok. I wrote in my diary:

> *Tomorrow's the big test – six hours minimum and hope the weather's okay.*

Although I was at the airport early next morning, 13 May, it seemed to take forever to finally get under way. I was anxious because of a forecast Tempo (bad weather) that was expected in Bangkok in about nine hours and I wanted to get there before it. Several young employees from Air Traffic Control had come to see me off and ask a few questions. It was a friendly gesture, but on departure, I preferred to be alone so that I could concentrate solely on my preparations for the flight and carefully go through all my checks.

As I turned out over the Andaman Sea after takeoff, at a height of between 200 and 300 feet, I felt something whizz over my head. Straightaway I thought of the fuel cap and felt sick and ashamed that I could have done this twice. Obviously in my haste to get away, because of the forecast weather and the small send-off party, I had failed to carry out my checks properly which included making sure the fuel cap was secure.

It's impossible to see the fuel cap from the pilot's seated position in the rear cockpit, but in order to assess the situation, I felt compelled to confirm that the cap had, in fact, gone. And so I undid my seat belt and shoulder harness and carefully half stood up on my seat, while controlling the stick with my fingertips. This was a delicate operation as my feet were also momentarily off the rudder pedals. A huge blast of air hit me as I exposed myself to the slipstream and the velcro fastener on one side of my life jacket (worn around my neck) was ripped apart in the process, allowing a yellow, deflated air bag to fall out and flap around. I quickly sat down again, but not before having managed to, indeed, see that the fuel cap was missing. As soon as I hit the seat a cold chill went through me as I realised that this circus act might well have had disastrous consequences, with *Margery* hurtling on towards Bangkok – without me! I firmly vowed, there and then, never to try that stunt again.

After spending the next few minutes tidying myself up and resecuring the life jacket, I weighed up my options and figured there were two. The first, and most obvious, was to return to Phuket, which would have saved any further worry. My second and preferred option was to look for suitable landing points ahead with a view to continuing on to Bangkok and if fuel was getting low, I could divert to one of those aerodromes. I theorised that with a full top tank, perhaps a quarter to one third of the contents would be sucked out into the atmosphere rather quickly and then stabilise. And so I devised a plan: if the fuel contents were below a certain minimum level by the time I was abeam Chumphon, one of my predetermined alternates, about two-and-a-quarter hours away, then I would land at that point. There was also an airfield at Surat Thani, just one hour ahead, if the fuel drop was more dramatic. Otherwise, I would continue on to Bangkok. Fortunately, all went according to plan and I did not have to carry out an emergency landing. My eyes remained transfixed, though, by the fuel gauge for almost the entire six hours, and I was careful when transferring fuel from the auxiliary to the top tank not to fill it any more than half to avoid further loss.

Despite the anxiety of my fuel problem, I managed to take in the picturesque countryside en route to my first waypoint, Surat Thani, 8NM south-west of the Gulf of Thailand. I was following a series of parallel, knife-edged, jungle-covered ridges. At one point, I was level with the top of one of these – less than a mile

*Courtesy The West Australian*

*Words of encouragement from His Excellency Major General Michael Jeffery, AC MC Governor of Western Australia*

*Courtesy The West Australian*

*Departure time with Carol*

Courtesy Jock Hay

*Rear cockpit - the office*

Unknown

*Take-off to the west, Langley Park*

*Unknown*

*Farewell formation*

*Author*

*Wittenoom Gorge, Pilbara WA*

Author

*On finals, Derby WA*

Author

*Local school visit, Derby WA*

Author

*Troughton Island*

Author

*Terraced farming, Indonesia*

Author

*With ground handlers, Bali*

Author

*Mt Merapi & Ljen Crater,*
*9, 186 ft, Java*

Author

*Exiting the storm, Sumatra*

Author

*Hangar for a night, Palembang*

Author

*Off to market, Palembang*

Author

*On top for a while - Palembang to Singapore*

away, and marvelled, once more, at the raw beauty of nature. From Surat Thani, I flew on to Chumphon on the western coast of the Gulf before heading out into it.

Compounding my fuel problems was a fleeting hallucination I experienced after five hours of flying – three of which had been over water with no real horizon. I thought I could see several helicopters about two miles ahead and slightly above me. They turned out to be boats in the Gulf of Thailand! I soon straightened myself out – nil horizon flying can be very demanding.

The final thirty minutes after crossing the coast for Bangkok Airport was horrendous – heavy smog and a thunderstorm – a lot of buffeting and very poor visibility. I was forced to request radar vectoring to the airport as there was no chance of seeing it. The large runways didn't come into view until I was a mere 3-4NM away. I was cleared to land on runway 21R. Wind sheer and turbulence on finals made for an untidy landing, but at least I was down safely, and after six-and-a-quarter hours flying, one of my most dreaded legs was over. I had dreaded it because it was long, 399NM, and the majority of it over water. Also, that I would be landing at a large international airport and the pressures of possibly being vectored between huge commercial aircraft, such as the Boeing 747. I was an ant by comparison and knew I could be squashed just as easily.

Although it was not scheduled, I decided to take a rest day in Bangkok so that I could sort out my visa for Myanmar (previously Burma) and also try and have a fuel cap sent up from Perth on an overnight Qantas flight. I booked into the Amari Hotel (courtesy Malaysia Airlines) which was connected to the airport by a first floor, covered walkway above a busy road. After my tiring flight, this was most convenient and saved the usual loading and unloading of luggage to and from taxis, and, sometimes, lengthy drive to my accommodation. I had a very comfortable room for the night.

Bangkok is also known as Krung Thep – The City of Angels. It was founded in the late eighteenth century and with a population of approximately ten million, is one of the largest cities in the world. One of the first things I noticed about Bangkok, both from the air and on the ground, was the thick, greyish-brown smog that seems to continually blanket the city.

I spent most of my rest day organising my visa and catching up on some housekeeping – laundry, neatly repacking luggage and studying my planned track to Rangoon. I also rang brother John and received a call from Werner Buhlmann and John Douglas from the Royal Aero Club in Perth – it was great to hear familiar voices.

I hadn't made any prior arrangements for obtaining my visa for Myanmar and was hoping that it would be issued on the same day. Deng, a taxi driver, picked me up from my hotel and drove me to the Myanmar Embassy, arriving at around 12.45pm. The note on the door advised they were closed until 2.00pm, and so I had about an hour to kill. Deng took me to a café where we shared tea and cake and chatted.

The embassy was located in an old building with bare timber floorboards, and divided into a large waiting area and a few smaller offices. The waiting area was full of people standing around waiting their turn, and it didn't appear to be an orderly set-up at all. I observed that most applicants had loose passport photos which they handed over the counter along with their paperwork. I had no photos and now being well into the afternoon, started to feel that my chances of obtaining a visa today were slim. I decided the only way was to try and bluff my way through.

When I eventually reached the counter, I told the embassy employee that I didn't come under either their Tourist or Business classifications and, in addition to my passport, proceeded to produce my AOPA air-crew badge (Aircraft Owners and Pilots Association) plus a small newspaper cutting of my trip from a

Penang newspaper. I said that I was really transiting aircrew and could I proceed to Myanmar on that basis, as it was imperative that I be allowed to leave in the morning. The employee stared down at my pathetic credentials on the counter and then straight back to me with an expressionless face and unblinking eyes. It seemed to be an eternity before he said anything and I started to get a sinking feeling. What was he thinking? Then I noticed his stony expression start to soften and in a quiet but clear voice he said, "Come with me." I was shown into the office of the Second Secretary of the Embassy, Soe Han, who looked no more than thirty. After I told my story once more he was totally sympathetic and stamped my passport with a Gratis Visa and no fees to pay. He also waived the usual requirement to cash US$300 (or equivalent currency) into Burmese currency on arrival. He told me that Gratis Visas were rarely given. I felt honoured and greatly relieved to have this outcome and let him know how grateful I was.

I was up early the following morning, keen to get to the airport and collect the replacement fuel cap and the additional engine oil that April had air-freighted from Perth. I was pleased to hear that these items had arrived, but getting my hands on them wasn't going to be easy. Since it was a Saturday, I was advised I would have to wait until Monday when the customs officer responsible for clearing fuel and oil products would be back on duty – he (apparently) was the only one who could release the oil. So I said to the official, "Well, you can keep the oil, just give me the fuel cap."

"No sir", he replied. "You see, the oil and fuel cap are one consignment and cannot be broken".

I was furious at this seemingly nonsensical reasoning and could hardly contain myself, but the Thai ground handling agent standing with me, seeing my anger, quickly pulled me aside and advised: "Customs people in Bangkok are very powerful and even get enjoyment at seeing people get upset." He advised me to look unperturbed and try to smile. I made a final request for just the fuel cap and spent the next three hours sitting under the wing of *Margery* on the tarmac, waiting for a decision. For Bangkok, it was a beautiful clear morning and I felt completely frustrated that I couldn't take advantage of it.

With the fuel cap fitted and the oil left behind in the Custom's compound, I finally took off at 11.20am, concerned at the cloud build-up in the distance. What worried me most was crossing the broad Dawna Range – a series of ridges north-east and parallel to Bilauktaung Range that run between Thailand and Myanmar. I knew how formidable this mountain range could be, particularly if the weather turned nasty. This particular section had been notorious since the pioneering flights of the 1920s and 1930s. I had calculated that about two hours of the total six-hour flight would be across the mountains and had promised myself that if the weather deteriorated within the first half hour of the mountain crossing, I would return to Bangkok. It turned out to be just manageable, with a cloud base of 4,500 to 5,000 feet and several mountain peaks 3,000 to 5,000 feet plus.

The Srinagarind Dam on the Mae Klong (River Kwai) was a beautiful sight in its rugged mountain setting. En route to the dam, my track had taken me to within 10NM of Kanchanaburi and the River Kwai. The infamous bridge had been built over the river near Kanchanaburi by the prisoners of the Japanese during World War II. Its purpose was to carry a railway line which became known as the 'death railway' and it is estimated some 16,000 prisoners and many more Asian workers died during the course of construction of both the bridge and railway line.

The mountain ridges were mostly covered in deep emerald vegetation, with areas of brown, barren rock visible in between. The colours were clearly discernible even though I was looking through a pale blue haze. Looking farther ahead, the browns and greens began to disappear as the haze intensified, until finally, the whole landscape, including the sky, had taken on a blue-grey appearance. It was surreal. Small settlements were scattered here and there in the fertile valleys, but overall there was very little sign of life. I was wary about crossing from Thailand into Myanmar on account of reported border clashes, which seemed to be increasing. My main concern was a pot-shot from a rebel's rifle. This wasn't just a fanciful worry on my part, as I later learnt in Rangoon that this could indeed have been a possibility, given the relatively low altitude I was flying. This had been the fate of Sir Alan Cobham's mechanic, A.B. Elliott, on a flight to Australia in a DH50J in 1926. When flying between Baghdad and Basra he was shot by an Arab and died later that day in a hospital in Basra.

I was somewhat relieved to finally get over the mountains, but then ran into rain showers on the other side and did my best to weave around them. As I headed out across the Gulf of Martaban from Moulmein, the water below appeared calm, but in the distance there was, once again, the dreaded sight of dark rain clouds which seemed to grow progressively larger and thicker the closer I got. At one point, I contemplated turning back to Moulmein, but finally decided it was sufficiently safe to continue on. I had my intentions relayed to Rangoon by Captain Norman Jameson of Zimex Aviation (Swiss) who happened to be flying a Twin Otter in the near vicinity. Just before I reached the other side of the Bay, the weather deteriorated and I flew through heavy showers and poor visibility for the next half hour or so. I was very relieved to finally make Rangoon (Yangon), although I got a flat tyre on landing.

Immigration processing was somewhat intimidating – seven white clad officials huddled around a trestle table in a small room firing questions at me. Once they realised what my trip was about, I was allowed to leave.

My first impression of Rangoon, or at least the airport, was the strong military presence – there were army personnel everywhere. Within minutes of climbing from the cockpit, I noticed a Burmese man in his mid-thirties following me. He was fairly tall, of slim build and dressed in civilian clothes. Slung over his shoulder was a video camera and in his hands a 35mm camera. He started filming me immediately, mainly using his video camera – even getting my luggage out of the baggage compartment and checking the oil. He didn't say anything and kept within about 20 feet of me. I presumed he was acting in an official capacity as a security officer, though found his presence very intimidating and wondered what on earth could appear sinister about my flying an old biplane from Australia to England.

When I enquired about purchasing Avgas (100 octane), the ground handling agent advised me it was very difficult to obtain in Rangoon and that none was available at the airport. Anyway, he said he would make enquiries and try to find a quantity for me.

While cleaning the engine bay and belly of *Margery* of excess oil, a duty I religiously carried out at the end of each day's flying, an elderly Burmese man came up to me saying he had recognised the Tiger Moth from some distance away. He mentioned he had worked on them during the Second World War and was obviously nostalgic as he slowly walked around *Margery* taking in every detail.

I asked a taxi driver to take me to a reasonable hotel and he recommended the Ramada, which wasn't far from the airport. On the way to the hotel, my face felt as though it was on fire and when I finally checked it out in a mirror, was horrified to see a bright red mask – since the day had been overcast, I'd made the fatal mistake of not applying enough sunscreen and was now going to pay the consequences. In fact, the following morning, after a restless night's sleep, I felt ill. I put it down to a combination of what I had eaten and my bad sunburn. Getting showered and dressed was an effort in itself, but because of the onset of the monsoon, I wanted to get the flat tyre repaired and push on as soon as possible to Chittagong in Bangladesh. Richard, a Canadian aircraft engineer who was one of a small party who had greeted me on arrival, drove me to a tyre repair shop, a ramshackle affair consisting of rough wooden poles with a canvas canopy at the front, old sheet iron cladding on the back and sides, and an earthen floor. The problem was a fretted valve stem which had to be cut out of the tube and a new one vulcanised in its place – an excellent job for the princely cost of 300 Kyat (one US dollar).

I returned to the airport with my mended tyre at around 11.00am and within a short time, *Margery* was standing on her own wheels again. The ground handler told me that he hadn't been able to locate any Avgas and the only fuel he could find was a 44-gallon drum of 80/87 octane, with a January, 1997 delivery date stamped on it. The fact that it was sixteen months old concerned me, but I decided to take it anyway so that I could move on. Since it was 80/87 octane I figured there was still sufficient Avgas remaining in *Margery's* tanks to pep it up a little. The 44-gallon drum soon arrived and was wheeled alongside *Margery* on a hand-pulled trolley. It was apparent the drum was once a light blue colour, but now covered in rust.

Before transferring the fuel to *Margery* via a hand pump, a sample was drawn into a glass jar and given to me to inspect. I checked it for clarity, colour and smell and that no water was present, and then told them to proceed. Three men assisted with the refuelling operation, including one of them holding up a black umbrella to stop rain entering the drum. The whole process ended up taking forty-five minutes and it was now after midday.

The security officer was watching me again today, though he eased the tension a little by talking to me. He mentioned that he was employed by the government for security purposes and had been recently assigned to follow crew movements and the events surrounding the aborted around-the-world balloon flight by Bertrand Piccard of Switzerland, in his craft *Breitling Orbiter*

*2.* He and his co-pilot, Andy Nelson, had departed Switzerland on 28 January 1998. Reaching the Far East, they were initially denied entry into Chinese airspace. At that point, they abandoned their around-the-world attempt and decided to try and break the time aloft record. They finally landed at Sitkwin Minhla, 130km north of Rangoon. Their flight of 9 days, 17 hours and 55 minutes covering a distance of 8,473km was a world record.

At the end of our conversation, he promised to give me some photos he had taken of me and *Margery* tomorrow, if we had not already departed.

The flight to Chittagong would take at least six hours and I knew I would be cutting it fine to get there by nightfall. And so I decided to delay my departure until the next day, a blessing in disguise, as it enabled me to have a couple of hours sleep in the afternoon, which I really needed.

Late in the day, I met up with Harry Hanlan, the chief pilot with Ken Borek Air Ltd, who flies the company's Twin Otter based in Rangoon and who happened to be staying at the same hotel. I had briefly spoken with him after my arrival the previous day. Harry was a thick-set, neatly presented American in his mid-fifties who had a brusque, no-nonsense manner about him. He obviously enjoyed his flying role in this remote part of the world and ran his operation with an iron-fist, as his not-all-that-happy trainee first officer later confided. Even so, he had a grudging respect for Harry.

The first officer then arrived and the three of us went to a restaurant, a short walk from the hotel, and dined in a raised outdoor area. Harry knew the restaurant owner and the food, although simple, was excellent. We spent a very pleasant hour eating and exchanging stories. I returned to my hotel room feeling revitalised and ready to tackle tomorrow.

# Chapter 6

## RANGOON TO CALCUTTA

**Days 23-27** - 18 May 1998 to 22 May 1998

Then was thunderstorm activity during the night and it rained heavily. A few drops even found their way into the fuel bowl drain on *Margery*. It was Monday 18 May and at breakfast, Harry Hanlan, who had many years of experience in the area, told me that this was the onset of the monsoon and that I should move on as quickly as possible.

I lodged my flight plan and obtained a weather report from the control tower – a rather old four-storey structure with many windows, pale cream walls and dark red roof. It was poorly appointed and dirty, but the weather man was precise and accurate with his forecast saying that the low pressure system in the Bay of Bengal was moving very slowly and that, although I would get some bad weather to start with, it should be reasonable at my destination, Chittagong. I was also informed it was highly probable this low pressure system would develop into a cyclone.

While preparing *Margery* for the flight, the security agent came across and gave me the photos as he had promised. There were three small, black and white prints taken of myself and *Margery* and they would serve as a fitting reminder of my time here in Rangoon. Following a brief, friendly conversation, it was time to swing *Margery*'s propeller.

Heading westwards towards Gwa, there was heavy cloud around and my course took me over the southern end of the Arakan Range, approximately 2,000 feet high, which had cloud sitting almost on top of it. There was a 500 feet to 1,000 feet clear layer between that and a higher cloud layer at about 3,500 feet, so I flew between the two. I was pleased to reach Gwa on the eastern coast of the Bay of Bengal with its single bitumen runway directly below me, and then proceeded northwards towards Sandoway and Sittwe.

Shower activity increased reducing visibility and I thought I was in for another of those days. Looking out to my left across the Bay of Bengal, I noticed a massive, dark grey cloud mass which appeared to be right down to sea level, and I knew that this was the cyclone I had been warned about. I kept a close eye on it as I headed up the coast, but fortunately, I was a safe distance from it. Around the halfway mark of this leg, the local weather started to clear. One positive effect of the cyclonic cell was the wind generated at its extremities, resulting in a 30 knot tailwind and a ground speed of 100 knots.

Just past the town of Cox's Bazar I made contact with an American airline captain who obligingly passed on my current position and ETA to Chittagong Tower. Although my landing was a good one, when I shut down the engine, I knew I had a problem when it ran on for another 20-30 seconds with the switches off. Pre-ignition was my first thought – a condition whereby an abnormally high build-up of carbon residue on the cylinder heads becomes red hot and continues to fire the engine with the switches off until it cools sufficiently. The cause of the carbon build-up can be poor quality fuel and so the only solution was to drain the remaining fuel and refill with fresh Avgas. But first I had to endure another rather tense meeting with a panel of white-clad Bangladeshi Customs officials. As in Rangoon, once the nature of my journey was explained and I showed them some newspaper cuttings from previous stops, they realised that I was obviously not a threat and eased up on the questions.

After two hours at the airport, the intense heat began to affect me. My mouth was dry, flying suit saturated with perspiration and energy sapped. As I finished climbing the seventy or so steps to the control tower to lodge my flight plan for the next day, I thought I was going to fall down at any moment. "Please get me some water," I tried to ask calmly to a young airport employee who was accompanying me. But he obviously didn't realise the urgency of the situation and said he would obtain some shortly. By this time I was desperate and blurted out, "Quickly, I need water now, right now!" He raced off and returned in a few minutes with one and a half litres in plastic bottles. I re-hydrated quickly and from that moment on carried water wherever I went.

It had been a long, hot and tiring day and it was such a relief to get out of my flying suit and have a shower. Feeling refreshed and wanting to stretch my legs, I asked the clerk at reception about going for a walk – was it safe? He said I should be okay, but not to venture too far and not to walk at night. With that, I headed off into the street with no destination in mind – just to have a bit of a look around.

It was crowded and obviously not a tourist area. Dressed only in a T-shirt, shorts and sneakers, I must have stood out like a sore thumb, especially with my lily-white legs! Within the space of five minutes, I was caught up in a throng of people who seemed to be going in all directions: there was no order to this pedestrian traffic. And then I felt a tug on my shirt sleeve. I spun around and was confronted by a woman of around forty. She was dressed in rags and her hair matted. The skin on her face was lined and deeply tanned and she had prominent cheek bones. She was standing very close to me and her deep brown eyes looked straight into mine. Her hand was turned upwards and in a firm, husky voice she asked for money. I was startled to say the least, and instantly rejected her, gesturing that I had no money on me, which was true. This seemed to infuriate her and she let out with a low hissing sound which I gathered was an expression of disgust. She then moved on. Although a short and rather harmless incident, it shook me up a little and I felt decidedly uncomfortable out in the streets on my own. Within the space of fifteen minutes, I was back in my hotel, feeling guilty and disappointed that I had not helped this poor woman.

Reaching Chittagong was something of a milestone, for, since leaving Perth, it had been a long, steady climb northwards and now, at last, I could start moving westwards in earnest – that much closer to England. Crossing India was my next priority and I had a feeling it was going to be four hot, arduous days.

I was up at 4.30am next morning, 19 May, keen to reach Calcutta before the cyclone in the Bay of Bengal got any closer. On the way to the airport, I could see that the weather was deteriorating and the meteorological report soon confirmed that.

All I could do was sit and wait at the airport and hope that conditions would improve.

The airport manager, Mr Anwar, a lean, well-groomed man of around fifty with dark piercing eyes, spoke impeccable English. He exuded an air of quiet control which gave me confidence in dealing with him. Around mid-afternoon, I was summoned to his office on the upper level of an old brick and concrete building. Three or four of his staff worked around a large table facing him and I sat next to them. He offered me tea, the forerunner of numerous cups of tea at the airport over the next couple of days. It was always the same – black and sweet – you were not asked, "How do you take it?" After the first two cups or so, I began to enjoy it.

Mr Anwar's mood at the first meeting was sombre as he explained that there were strong fears the cyclone might reach the airport. He related that a similar cyclone had struck the Chittagong area in April 1991, killing over 30,000 people. In addition, the resultant tidal surge completely flooded the airport and forty military aircraft were lost. With an elevation of just twelve feet and its proximity to the Bay of Bengal, Chittagong is very susceptible to flooding. For that reason, the entire Bangladeshi jet fighter fleet had been evacuated to Dhaka, the capital, some 125km north, early this morning. The only aircraft remaining were a fleet of helicopters that had been parked and tied down on specially built concrete ramps approximately twelve feet off the ground.

Mr Anwar now strongly urged me to follow the example of the fighter aircraft and evacuate to Dhaka. There was no way *Margery* could be tied down on one of the concrete ramps as the force of a wind even close to a cyclone would tear her to pieces. I explained to him the winds were already too strong for me to depart, and that I would have to take my chances here. I asked if I could park *Margery* in one of the numerous vacant hangars, but the problem was that, although the military and civilian aircraft operators shared the airport, the military facilities, including administration buildings, hangars, etc, were out of bounds to non-military personnel.

After further pleading from Mr Anwar to evacuate with *Margery*, he finally conceded that I was staying put, no matter what, and then went and sought permission for me to relocate to one of the military hangars. An hour later, I taxied *Margery* to a large open-fronted hangar and parked her at the very rear of the building. I tied her down to heavy steel loops set in the concrete floor and then left for the hotel with Sohelul Huq, a young manager of the Padma Oil Company, who had refuelled *Margery*. Sohelul understood my concerns and did his best to reassure me that everything would be all right.

At the Agraba Hotel, the weather progressively worsened and out of my window large palm trees were bending right over and the torrential rain was horizontal. The lights periodically went off and on and the wild sound of the wind and rain, and buffeting of the windows, is something I shall never forget. The streets were awash and, with the exception of a few brave souls determined to reach their destination, deserted. I was restless and anxious.

Night now descended, and although not feeling particularly hungry, I decided to head downstairs to dinner. If nothing else, it would be a distraction for a while.

Returning to my room, some time later, the storm was still raging outside. I lay on top of my bed with eyes half-closed and had visions of *Margery* drowned under twelve feet of water: I felt absolutely helpless. And then the phone rang at 12.50am. It was the airport and the concerned voice at the other end told me that the storm would "attack" the airport at 4.00am, flooding was expected and "you must move your aeroplane". Where he wanted me to move it to at the height of a storm, I didn't know and could only think of the elevated concrete ramps.

I quickly got dressed and with not a taxi to be found anywhere, was lucky to be given a lift by a man and his young son who had been asleep in their battered old van in front of the hotel. They didn't appear overly enthusiastic about being awoken by a hotel employee to give me assistance, but I was most grateful and endeavoured to make amends with a healthy reward at the end of the journey. Apart from anything else, I felt genuine compassion for their plight – it would appear that this dilapidated van was their home and probably their only real possession.

At the airport, the strong winds and rain persisted and I had considerable difficulty trying to gain access to *Margery*. I finished up in a small command post on the perimeter of the base and spoke to the officer in charge by telephone. Although sympathetic to my fear of losing *Margery* to sea flooding, he made it very clear that, given the severity of the storm and the fact that this was a military base, I was not to proceed any further and should return to the hotel. I had no option but to comply with his command and arrived back at 2.20am. Soon after, the same officer phoned to assure me that *Margery* would be safe and to stop worrying, and to try and get some sleep.

The storm raged throughout the night and continued until midday the following day. I hardly slept a wink. Mr Anwar called me at around 1.00pm to advise that the cyclone had passed and fortunately, Chittagong Airport had been spared. I was over the moon. Sohelul then arrived to take me to the airport. On the way I saw widespread damage – trees blown down, thatched cottages and street side stalls destroyed and a large steel bulk fuel storage tank, which was under construction, stoved in on one side by the force of the wind.

*The Bangladesh Observer* (Thursday, May 21, 1998) reported that as a result of the cyclone, fourteen people were killed and eighteen fishermen were missing. Wind speeds of up to 160kph were reported near the coast. The article also reported that "A preliminary estimate showed about 5,000 Kutcha and Semi-Pucca homes in the coastal areas of Banshkhali, Sitakundu and Anwara were either blown away or razed to the ground." The article continued: "Waterlogging by heavy downpour at the Chittagong Airport has been cleared and the port is now fit for operation."

At the airport Mr Anwar came with me to inspect *Margery.* It was a great relief to see her in one piece, unscathed.

The following day, rain and low cloud persisted and I had no alternative but to wait until it improved. I carried out a few minor jobs on *Margery,* but as there was no suitable oil available at the airport, I would have to wait until reaching Jamshedpur in India to carry out the mandatory 100 hourly inspection and service. The Maintenance Release document showed that *Margery* was within the legal limits with still 5 hours to run until the required work, and I had calculated I could reach Jamshedpur and stay just within this limit. Also, I preferred to carry out the 100 hourly inspection at the smaller and quieter Jamshedpur Airport rather than at the large and busy international airport at Calcutta.

During the day, I drank more tea with Mr Anwar and then with Sohelul in the Padma Oil Company office. This was a small building detached from the main airport structures and had a definite charm and character about it. It appears to have been built in the 1930s, most probably by the British, and had attractive art deco features. Adding to this charm was the way in which the office was run. Sohelul was the only occupant of the office and his five staff were housed in a small shed at the rear. At the press of a button, near Sohelul's desk, one of them would come running – literally – and present himself to receive instructions. These instructions were never given civilly, but were barked at the seemingly terrified individual standing before him. At even the slightest mistake, Sohelul would fly into a rage. Although somewhat amused at his style of management, I was also disturbed that people could be treated in this way. Beneath his tough façade though, there seemed to be a softer and kinder side to Sohelul when he talked of his young family and the bleak future that lay ahead of them in Bangladesh. He even asked about emigrating to Australia, which to him, would be a dream come true.

Sohelul organised a lift for me back to my hotel and I recorded the experience in my diary:

> *The ride back through the city was an absolute hell drive*
> *– dozens and dozens of old dilapidated trucks, 3 wheel*
> *Vespa vehicles, rickshaws, etc. The tooting of horns*
> *was incredible and the traffic, to my mind, wildly out*
> *of control – near misses by the second. Exhaust fumes*
> *were choking. And so I said goodbye to Sohelul and will*
> *always remember him as being a most interesting fellow*

*and, of course, his kindness to me.*

Back at the hotel I met a Scotsman, Tom Grieve, in the lobby. He told me that he and two Englishmen had recently flown around the coast of Australia in motorised hang-gliders, and had also visited the Royal Aero Club of Western Australia. What a surprise to bump into a total stranger so far from Australia who had actually visited my flying club!

I got up at 5.00am the next morning, 22 May, and managed to contact Carol, who was now in Canada, still en route to England to meet me. We hadn't spoken to each other for well over a week and it was reassuring for each of us that we were both okay.

At the airport I once again made the long climb up the tower to obtain a weather report and lodge my flight plan. The weather was only just reasonable, but as I didn't want to stay a day longer, I decided to go. A group of Air Force personnel were present as I carried out the pre-flight on *Margery*. They asked a number of questions about my flight and we even had a bit of a laugh, which helped to relieve the ever-present, pre-take-off nerves.

A 12 knot crosswind was blowing as I commenced my take-off run and the cloud base was around 2,000 feet. I immediately felt apprehensive flying at only 1,500 to 2,000 feet as I contemplated the water crossing to India, and for a few moments considered returning to Chittagong. There was, once again, that awful, sickening feeling in the stomach that I might be heading into danger that was avoidable by turning back, but I quickly countered the thought with the knowledge that the weather was supposed to improve the further west I flew. I had no desire to return to Bangladesh if I could possibly help it, and reaching India was my number one goal for now. After thirty-five minutes of flying, I passed just to the south of Sandwip Island and my weather-related fears diminished.

Then it was across the expansive Mouths of the Ganges with

their numerous small islands and channels. At precisely 11.50am local time I crossed the town of Sumag on the Indian border and prepared myself for the final run into Calcutta. On approach to the airport, the conditions were hazy and being a rather flat, featureless landscape, nothing particularly stood out from the air. Also, arriving from the east, I couldn't see anything of the city, a few miles west of the airport. After some 3.2 hours of flying I was on finals for Runway 19L, which was huge – 11,900 feet in length. I was happy with my landing given the hot, blustery wind that was blowing.

Sisir Mukhopadhyay, the senior Traffic Superintendent for Air India, came out to meet me as I was shutting down. He was a short, silver-haired man in his mid-fifties, with a neat appearance and a quiet, efficient manner – just what I needed.

In Chittagong the night before, I had decided that if I made good time to Calcutta, I would land, obtain customs and immigration clearances and push on for Jamshedpur. As I had landed in Calcutta at 12.25pm local time I had ample time to proceed with this plan, but I determined I would need to leave no later than 2.30pm in order to reach Jamshedpur in reasonable light.

Aware of my plan, Sisir went out of his way to help me, and after approximately one-and-a-half hours, I had the necessary clearances and my flight plan was lodged. *Margery* was refuelled and all that remained was permission from the Airport Controller. We walked through a series of passageways and took an antiquated, steel-caged lift to a couple of floors above. Sisir led me into a huge, dingy office with high ceilings and electric fans circulating the warm, humid air. In one corner the small wiry figure of the Airport Controller sat at a cluttered desk. Several employees were standing at the desk, each apparently waiting their turn to have a discussion with him, and my overall impression was that things were a little chaotic.

Within a short space of time, Sisir and I were standing at the desk and Sisir formally asked the question, could I now proceed to Jamshedpur? Without seeming to move his head, the Controller raised his narrowed, glaring eyes to me and that, combined with the expressionless look on his face, told me what the answer was going to be. It was no. He was sticking to my overflight clearance, which stated I was departing for Jamshedpur the next day, 23 May 1998. When I tried to argue the point that it was just a matter of a simple amendment, he rang Head Office in Delhi. To my utter dismay I could hear him virtually putting words into the Delhi official's mouth to reject my request. Although disappointed, I decided it was no use arguing with these people. The Controller was obviously an inflexible man who seemed to have taken an instant dislike to me.

So I lodged my flight plan for tomorrow to depart around 6.30am. I was keen to get to Jamshedpur to carry out the 100 hourly maintenance on *Margery* which was now due. The weather was also looking favourable. My final diary note read:

> *Had soup (asparagus), fish and chips for dinner. Going to bed early, have to be at airport by 5.30am. Feel very tired, but really pleased to be in India. Will be in bed by 9.00pm.*

71

# Chapter 7

# CALCUTTA TO KARACHI

**Days 28-32** - 23 May 1998 to 27 May 1998

I was awake at 4.30am, 23 May, and at the airport by 5.20am to be met by Sisir. After completing another pile of forms, I was ready to depart at 6.30am. When I requested permission to start *Margery's* engine, however, the tower advised me that my flight plan had been suspended on account of poor visibility, i.e. it was currently 2.5km to 3km and when it reached 5km I could fly.

I eventually departed at 10.30am. Visibility was still marginal for the first one-and-a-half hours and I was forced to remain at 2,000 feet on account of the low cloud base. As with the day before, the landscape was grey and bleak owing to the cloud and haze, and my only interest was in reaching Jamshedpur. With only a few nautical miles to run, I crossed the muddy Subarnarekha River. The city of Jamshedpur was just out to my left and straight ahead, the airport, with its single bitumen-sealed runway, was clearly visible. After an uneventful flight of 2.4 hours I landed just prior to 1.00pm.

The ground temperature was extreme. A few well-wishers came out to greet me. Jamshedpur Airport had been used for training purposes during the Second World War and is now privately owned. It is very small with just a single runway and a handful of old buildings and hangars. Tatanagar Aviation Pty Ltd occupied one of the hangars and willingly offered their facilities to enable me to carry out the 100 hourly. Although clearly a small and basic operation, the company appeared to be excellently run and had a total complement of around eight, including the chief engineer. Two of the maintenance staff were men in their sixties who had worked on Tiger Moths in India some forty years ago. They were keen to assist and I took an instant liking to the place: there was something about it that struck a chord in me. We decided to carry out the maintenance the next morning.

Of further interest was a small flying school which operated out of the hangar with two single-engine Cessna Aircraft. It was run by a thirty-year-old CFI (chief flying instructor) who had come up from Madras two weeks before to try and build up a training programme. There were five students in all, including two young girls. I told them about my daughter April, who was learning to fly. All of the students addressed the CFI as 'sir' and he barked orders at them on a regular basis – to help push an aircraft out, turn it around, change the battery, etc. They literally ran everywhere – not quite like the Royal Aero Club of WA, back home.

I wasn't happy with the hotel I had booked into earlier at the suggestion of a taxi driver. The room I was given was small, poorly appointed and not particularly clean. If I'd been staying one night, I would have put up with it but as it was two nights, I decided to find something better. Mentioning this to one of the student pilots, he recommended The Kanchan Guest House and happily helped me to change over. It cost me a day's tariff – about A$30, but I could live with that, especially as my room in the alternative hotel was comfortable and clean.

That evening I ate a simple meal in the hotel and then retired to my room to reorganise some of my luggage, pull out clothing to be washed and go over my flight plans.

As darkness fell, I could hear music and pulling back the curtains of my first floor window was surprised to see that I was next to an amusement park. Brightly coloured lights adorned the entrance and in the centre I could see the outline of a partially illuminated Ferris Wheel against the now black night sky. A steady trickle of people were arriving for their night of fun. The scene was a warm, happy one and I enjoyed watching it.

Jamshedpur, also known as Tatanagar, is a major iron and steel producing centre and has a population of over 500,000. Its major production items include motor vehicles, locomotive components and farming machinery. Although busy with traffic, the atmosphere of the city was relaxed and it was easy to move around.

The 100 hourly was carried out the following morning and concluded with a ground run at 12.30pm – the distinctive Gipsy sound was smooth and even. I spent most of the afternoon at the airport cleaning *Margery* and chatting with people; for a change, I wasn't under any pressure and could relax.

In the evening I was entertained by Mr Sanjay Singh, a director of Tata Steel, and his wife and several other invited guests at the Beldih Club for hors d'oeuvres and cold drinks. The exclusive Beldih Club was established in 1922 and is situated on just under five acres of land, which includes a golf course. Although it has been progressively modernised over the years, there is still an English colonial feel to the place, which added to the atmosphere. The Beldih Club caters well to the business fraternity and Tata Steel has been its major corporate patron from the beginning.

Sanjay was also a pilot and the guests included the Chief Engineer from Tatanagar Aviation and an ex-Air Force pilot who had flown a number of legendary fighter aircraft including the MIG 21, Mirage and Jaguar. I thoroughly enjoyed the evening and the hospitality that was extended to me. Once back at the hotel, I started to worry about the long flight next day to Nagpur, and the extreme heat – around 45°C.

I got up at five o'clock the following morning, which was Monday 25 May, and the thirtieth day of my journey. Although I didn't know it at the time, this also marked the halfway point of the total number of days it took to complete the journey.

At the airport, the Chief Engineer gave me a lift on the back of his Vespa scooter to lodge my flight plan. Once again, I had to fill out a multitude of forms, and to add to my frustration, the Tower Controller rejected my flight plan saying I must fly the designated air transport route. After twenty minutes or so of solid reasoning, emphasising the safety factor, I managed to convince him to allow me to fly my proposed VFR (Visual Flight Rules) route, which was over a number of towns and airfields marked on my chart. Refuelling was completed after another forty-five minutes and my proposed departure time of 8.00am had blown out to 10.00am. This made me feel angry, but on a happier note, there were about twenty or so people to see me depart.

With fuel tanks filled to capacity, I commenced my take-off run. Despite applying full throttle, after 300 metres I was still firmly on the ground. The already high temperature had obviously thinned the air, making flight difficult, but then just as I was about to abort the take-off, the runway sloped away and *Margery* gently, and ever so slowly, departed the ground. This was my most sluggish take-off to date and not a good feeling. It took forty-five minutes to coax *Margery* up to the assigned cruising altitude of 6,000 feet.

The tacho started to play up about three hours into the flight, with the needle swinging wildly from side to side – it even managed a couple of 360° turns. Watching this performance for the next thirty minutes was distracting and I was relieved when the tacho finally died, the needle now pointing permanently to the six o'clock position: I was 80NM from Nagpur. Until I could have it repaired, I would need to take great care not to over-rev the engine and would now have to rely upon engine sound, and of course the airspeed indicator. Although the tacho had been fully overhauled, they are known to break down occasionally, and it was therefore not totally unexpected.

About the same time as the tacho breaking, I started to feel tired and could feel myself dozing off. It took a great deal of effort to stay awake. Thinking of family and friends, doing fuel calculations, transferring fuel from one tank to another, having a sip of water and eating a biscuit, all seemed to help. But it was an awful experience while it was occurring and probably lasted about a quarter of an hour.

Another strange experience on this leg began around midday and continued for a couple of hours. It was the effect of strong thermals. Flying at 6,000 feet, *Margery* suddenly started to climb. I tried to correct with forward stick (that is to say, pushing the joystick forward) but we continued to rise. The altimeter now showed 7,000 feet and the wind forces, which were coming from behind, seemed very powerful. We were severely buffeted and I was concerned, not only about the damage that might be caused to the wings and tail, but indeed that they would remain intact. It was almost as if *Margery* was in the grip of a giant, invisible hand that was totally ignoring my input. It felt like being on a wild roller coaster ride and I badly wanted to get off. I found the only effective means to bring the situation back under reasonable control was to reduce power significantly. Although this affected my ground speed, it felt decidedly safer and more comfortable.

On reaching Nagpur, I had some difficulty in picking up the runway on account of the haze, and once on the ground, it was stifling hot – 47°C. My first task was to try and have my VFR flight plan approved for tomorrow. After climbing some sixty stairs of an old, and rather grubby, Control Tower, I encountered a not too obliging controller – it appeared I would be flying a revised route tomorrow.

Standing around in a sweat-saturated flying suit is not the most comfortable thing in the world and I was looking forward to throwing it off and having a shower. The handling agent recommended a hotel on the fringe of town, not far from the airport, and I arrived there at 5.00pm. I didn't venture into the main town. Before my long awaited shower, I first rang April at home to organise a tacho cable for me. The bedroom was stifling hot and it would be stretching the imagination to say that the air being pumped out by the antiquated, rattling air conditioner was cool. However, that was the least of my worries – I just needed a good night's sleep.

I felt dehydrated and made sure I drank plenty of bottled water. My food intake during today's flight had been limited to a couple of biscuits, as usual, though instead of looking forward to a good evening meal, as I generally did, tonight I didn't feel hungry at all. Perhaps it was the heat or because I was tired. So I settled for a simple rice dish and ate it in my room.

The day's flight had been a long 6.5 hours and not a particularly smooth run, but at least I was now halfway across India.

I arrived at the airport bright and early next morning, and after considerable discussion with the airport controller, I agreed to a direct track – Nagpur to Ahmedabad – 290°. This was an IFR (Instrument Flight Rules) route and not over the VFR (Visual Flight Rules) track I had worked out which would have taken me over several towns, including Indore which has its own airport. The IFR route afforded no such landmarks, nor offered the security of an airport or airfield along the way. There was a positive though, as Indian Airlines Ltd charged me only US$50 for handling charges.

Soon after leaving Nagpur, my backside started to ache, and although I'd experienced this on previous days, today it was more noticeable. In fact, the further I flew on this leg, the worse it became. There was little I could do to relieve the pain on account of the confined space in the cockpit and the impossibility of leaving the seat. The best I could do was wriggle around a little or take turns of leaning to one side and then to the other to momentarily relieve pressure on this obviously inflamed part of my anatomy.

Keeping an accurate fuel log, pumping fuel up to the top tank at regular intervals, having the occasional sip of water through the plastic tube and eating a biscuit or two were temporary distractions from my physical problem. On the brighter side, the weather was reasonable. I later noted in my diary:

> *Had good weather today – even some blue sky. Haze not so bad as in other parts of India. Had a badly aching backside though, and I think the long accumulated hours in the seat are starting to tell.*

It was most inhospitable country – hot and dry and sparsely vegetated. I noticed the occasional small settlement or town, but other than that, it was almost desert-like in appearance and had a remote feeling.

From the folded map on my knee and the drawn track, I could see that, just past the halfway mark of this leg, I would traverse the Narmada River. This was something to look forward to and would be a welcome break from the generally brown, bland landscape. In effect, it became a mini-goal and as I had found on a number of previous legs, it was a simple but effective means of breaking-up a long journey and adding some interest.

Right on cue I crossed the river, but then had to make sure that I did not violate the airspace of a designated military area (VAD 8) positioned just to the north in a mountain range, two-and-a-half hours from Ahmedabad.

The approach into Ahmedabad was similar to Nagpur in that I could not see much of the town on account of the haze. I landed close to 4.00pm and was greeted by a few local aviation enthusiasts. One had flown Tigers many years ago and another had worked on them. It was extremely hot (47°C) but there were a few formalities I needed to attend to before I could proceed to my lodgings. This was not one of my Malaysia Airlines sponsored stops and, as such, no accommodation had been prearranged. I just hoped that I could find somewhere comfortable, no matter how basic it might be. So long as I had a clean bed and a shower, and something to eat, that was all I needed: to date, that had been the case. After satisfying immigration requirements, I headed straight to the control tower to discuss my flight plan for tomorrow.

Prior to leaving Australia, I had pre-prepared basic flight plans for each leg based upon VFR (Visual Flight Rules) and using my TAS (True Airspeed) of just 50 knots. I adopted 50 knots instead of the usual 60 or 70 knots as a worst case scenario to ensure that I had ample fuel for each leg, i.e. in case of unpredictable headwinds, getting off course or, worst still, getting lost. The routes I had chosen took into account factors such as the topography of the land and the nearness of airports and towns en route. The idea was to plan as short and safe a route as possible.

And so I spent the next two hours arguing with airport officials dressed in their pristine, white cotton suits on why they should allow me to fly a safe VFR route instead of their preferred IFR route consisting of imaginary waypoints with names such as Sasro and Chor. This being the fourth day of my travels across India, you'd think I'd have learnt by now that reasoning with Indian officialdom was pointless, but I wasn't going to give up without a fight. They finally told me, "It is the IFR route or nothing."

When I asked to speak to someone in higher authority they rang the Director of Aviation in Delhi. Once again the answer was a flat "No", but before hanging up they asked would I like to speak to him. I said yes, and fighting hard to keep my emotions under control, I started to relate to the Director why I did not want to fly their chosen route. After listening to me for about forty-five seconds without saying a word in response, he hung up. That was it! I was enraged and let fly at the assembled group, not caring about the consequences: "Your Director's decision lacks logic and I think it is a disgrace to treat a visitor to your country as I've been treated!" I said. The officials were stunned by my sudden outburst and I was equally surprised to see several of them nodding their approval. For in fairness, I believe they knew what I was up against in flying such an old aircraft – as in the course of my argument I had directed their attention to *Margery*, clearly visible from the control tower in her parking bay below.

I continued: "What you are making me do is not in the best interests of safety. How can I navigate visually to an imaginary point on the ground? Your press would like to hear about this." There were several murmurs of approval and one official said, "Well yes, you should tell them." But they were clearly bound by the law makers in Delhi, and as on previous days, I had no choice but to yield to their decision.

I'd arrived in Ahmedabad at four o'clock and it was now seven in the evening and I was still not finished at the airport. For the next one-and-a-half hours I filled out form after form and the straw that nearly broke the camel's back (mine) was a customs official's insistence that we walk the one kilometre back to *Margery* to "seal up the aircraft". What a joke! How can you seal up a Tiger Moth? Well they did – the seal consisted of a small piece of white paper approximately 6 by 2 inches which was pasted across one edge of the pilot's door where it met the fuselage in the closed position, and then signed by the customs official. Unbelievable! It was a hot humid night, the top half of my flying suit was completely saturated with perspiration, and I was exhausted.

I loaded my gear into a taxi and finally arrived at a small hotel recommended by an airport employee at around nine o'clock.

Before having a shower, a quick meal and crashing into bed, I rang daughters April and Alison at home. After what I'd been through, their voices sounded heavenly and I could feel the tension leaving my body almost immediately. I slept soundly.

I arrived at the airport at 6.30am the following morning and obtained my custom's clearance, as I was finally departing India. I next visited the meteorological office and then climbed the eighty or so steps to the top of the control tower to lodge my flight plan. The atmosphere was totally different today and the Air Traffic Controllers couldn't do enough for me. This similarly applied to the ground handlers. Just as I was about to leave the tower, the phone rang, and the Controller said it was for me. What a pleasant surprise to hear my secretary Sunny's voice! She had my new Pakistan clearance number which was essential for me to enter the country. (I was carrying an outdated clearance which no doubt would have caused problems.) It was a stroke of luck that she managed to get through to the tower at all and also that I happened to be there at that precise moment.

After take-off, I slowly climbed to my assigned altitude of 6,500 feet, but on levelling out and settling into the cruise was disappointed that I was only achieving a ground speed of 55-60 knots. Whilst still in range of Ahmedabad radar, I requested and was granted a revised altitude of 4,500 feet. It was always a matter of experimenting quite early in the flight to determine which level had the most favourable winds. My ground speed immediately improved to 65-70 knots, which was the best I could hope to achieve and would provide an ample safety margin in relation to my fuel reserves.

A frustrating aspect of my Indian legs was that although I arrived at the airport at about six o'clock each morning, I never managed to get away for at least another three or four hours – it always took that long to complete all the formalities. Today was no exception and although I'd arrived a little later (6.30am), it was frustrating that I wasn't able to take off until 11.00am, which meant that I was flying at the hottest time of day in one of the hottest parts of the world.

The first forty-five minutes or so of the flight were reasonable, but then visibility started to deteriorate as a result of haze, and the landscape was becoming more barren by the minute. My flight chart for this region was stamped in bold letters, RELIEF DATA INCOMPLETE and, as I entered the region, LIMITS OF RELIABLE RELIEF INFORMATION. The ground below was a murky brown-grey colour and blended with the sky, which took on a similar hue, with no clearly defined horizon. The air was warm and dense, creating an eerie atmosphere. I was flying over the Rann of Kutch, a vast flood plain which is mostly covered by water from June to November. The murky brown-grey colour was extensive mud flats and today being 27 May, the presence of still, shallow water was already evident.

A chill went through me as I contemplated my chances of surviving a forced landing in such a forbidding area, and I quietly cursed the thoughtless officialdom that had made me fly this route. My preferred route encompassed similar country, but to a much lesser extent, and besides, it was direct, as opposed to the circuitous path and considerably longer distance I had been forced to travel. Crossing the border into Pakistan, a small, barren, mountain range with a spot height of 1,177 feet came into view. It was brown in colour, very rugged in appearance and rose sharply from the desert floor. I was soon passing directly over the top of it, admiring its stark beauty.

Further into the flight, I noticed a number of desert settlements and marvelled how anyone, or anything, could exist in such an environment. I wrote in my diary:

> I flew over some of the most desolate country I have ever
> flown across. At 4,500 feet I could feel the heat and just
> steadily flew along to the two designated IFR points,

*before turning for Karachi.*

The last IFR point was Chor, which left me with about a two-and-a-half hour run into Karachi. At the halfway mark of this leg, I passed within 10NM of Hyderabad Airport, but given the hazy conditions, which now had a dust component, I saw nothing but a brown, sandy landscape and then the distinctive feature of a large, dry river bed similarly coloured. From 45NM, I had been trying to make contact with Karachi Tower until at 30NM, a cheerful American voice came on the radio offering to relay my current position, altitude and ETA (estimated time of arrival). He was flying a homebuilt amphibian with a Frenchman and they were also heading for Karachi, with just a few miles to go.

The final half hour was a turbulent ride on account of the heat, but I did my best to hold *Margery* as steady as possible. On approach to the airport and just 4NM out, five kites passed beneath my starboard wing and I was thankful that I was just that much higher than they were. For most of the day's flight, I had flown at 4,500 feet and for the final stages, was provided with radar vectoring, gradually reducing height to 2,500 feet and then 1,000 feet. The visibility was so poor I didn't sight the airport until 4NM and was then given a straight-in approach on runway 25R – wind 270° at 15 knots. The intense heat and wind gusts didn't augur for a good landing, but I arrived - in a fashion. I taxied next to the big, yellow, twin-engined amphibian and thanked the pilot for relaying my radio call. They had also flown from Australia (Sydney) with their destination being France. We decided we would all have a beer when we reached Dubai, but unfortunately that did not eventuate.

It had been another long, tiring day with 5.9 hours in the cockpit, but it was also another sizeable chunk of the total journey behind me. My reward for today was the excellent Pearl

Continental Hotel, once again courtesy of Malaysia Airlines. I rang April and Alison back home to tell them I had arrived safely, and also spoke to my sister June who had rung to give me some moral support. Then it was a matter of checking everything for tomorrow, a light meal, and bed.

Karachi was chosen as the capital of Pakistan in 1947, and with a population of close to nine million, is its largest city. New building activity, including high-rise offices and apartments, was prevalent and the city had a vibrant feel to it.

Author

*Bangkok Airport - storm approaching*

Author

*Srinagarind Dam on River Kwai*

Author

*Refuelling, Rangoon*

Author

*Repairing Margery's tyre, Rangoon*

*Courtesy Airport Security Agent*

*Author, Rangoon Airport*

*Courtesy Airport Security Agent*

*Margery, Rangoon Airport*

Author

*Refuelling, Chittagong - cyclone on the way*

Author

*Tatanagar Aviation PVT LTD - staff Jamshedpur Airport*

Author

*With locals, Jamshedpur Airport*

Author

*Evelyn Brey, Secretary Dubai Flying Club*

*Author*

*Saudi Arabian Desert*

*Author*

*Ancient volcanic crater, Saudi Desert*

*Author*

*Author, Jeddah*

*Author*

*Nile River - Valley of the Kings in background*

Author

*Security guards and ground handler, Luxor*

Author

*Nile River near Luxor - a ribbon of green. En route to Alexandria*

# Chapter 8

# KARACHI TO BAHRAIN

**Days 33-37** - 28 May 1998 to 1 June 1998

Carol was my alarm clock this morning, 28 May. She phoned just after 5.00am and as we had not spoken for a while, there was a lot for both of us to open our hearts about in the limited time available. It gave us both a lift and would get us through the next five or six days when we would next talk.

At the airport, a policeman became suspicious as to my bona fides and what my mission was. The fact I was dressed in a flying suit and not wearing my captain's insignia might have had something to do with it. Despite the handling agent's best efforts, the policeman was not having a bar of my story, and I was ushered to a command post within the terminal building. It consisted of a single room measuring about fifteen feet by ten, with no windows, and containing just two small desks and chairs. There were three or four policemen standing around inside, and an officer in charge sitting at one of the desks. At one end of the room was the strange sight of a Pakistani man in his thirties, dressed in traditional flowing white robes, standing motionless facing the wall. His nose would have been barely two inches from it and his gaze was fixed on the plaster directly in front of him. The last time I saw something like this was back in primary school.

After ten minutes or so of waiting to speak to the officer in charge, I observed a khaki-clad policeman approach the apparent miscreant, still facing the wall, and standing close and side-on to him, proceed to berate him in a loud voice directly into his ear. He was then allowed to leave. Poor fellow, it was obviously only a minor misdemeanour he had committed within the airport confines, but I couldn't help but see the funny side of it. This then turned into the horrible thought that I might be subjected to similar treatment.

When it was my turn to be interviewed by the officer, he was surly and unsmiling, but faced with the wealth of evidence I had managed to scavenge from my bags – including photographs of *Margery*, newspaper cuttings and log book entries – I was able to convince him that my mission wasn't a national threat and I was allowed to leave.

I finally fired *Margery* up at 10.50am, and while sitting in the cockpit preparing to taxi, suddenly realised that I had left my Mountain Design jacket back at the hotel. This had become my favourite item of apparel, and although it would not be required in the intense heat of this particular leg, it certainly would be when I reached Europe.

There was no other option but to shut the engine down and see if someone would be kind enough to retrieve it from the hotel for me – it was important for me to now stay on the live side of the airport and not to have to deal with the awkward airport officialdom again if I were to go and collect it myself. The handling agents rang the hotel to say they would come and collect it, but the hotel manager wanted me to come. I noted in my diary:

> *What a joke, India all over again! After much arguing the hotel finally agreed to drop it out to the airport for me – took an hour and the hotel is only 15 minutes away. Once again I was very hot and agro.*

I finally got airborne at noon, and for the first forty minutes or so I was radar vectored out over the ocean around a restricted zone. When I was finally left to my own devices, I was confronted with a total loss of horizon as a result of heavy haze and increasing cloud cover. Nearest landfall at this point was some 25NM away on my right. For a time I was cloud-dodging at around 2,000 feet and keeping a wary eye on the Arabian Sea beneath me. But the situation wasn't improving at all, so I decided to move closer to the coast and try to sight some land.

A sickening feeling once again came over me as the visual cues that gave me my reference to the world below, and whether or not I was flying straight and level, were starting to disappear. With no artificial horizon, I was having to rely on basic instruments which made flying very demanding. The weather report I had obtained prior to departure indicated reasonable weather all the way to Gwadar, with the exception of haze. Obviously, this combination of cloud and haze was confined to the ocean areas, so it was vital that I regain visual contact with the coast. Rather than risk going below 1,500 feet at this point, I decided to try and climb above the cloud. But, in an almost teasing way, the cloud tops seemed to be getting higher and higher and I was having to concentrate hard on the instruments in front of me. I finally concluded that this was not going to work either, so I reduced height and went back to picking my way through the cloud and haze, all the time edging closer to the coast.

It was as if my eyes were on stalks as I strained to sight land, and what a relief when I eventually did! The apprehension and strain left me in an instant as I now headed up the coast line, passing over Ormara and Pasni Airfields along the way. Earlier, I had made contact with a commercial airliner (Pakistan 525) and asked the captain to relay my present position and estimate for Gwadar to Karachi Control. The reason for this was that I could not, at this point, make contact with Gwadar Tower, though I knew Karachi Control would have the means to do so.

The landscape was an eerie grey-brown colour and appeared to be totally devoid of vegetation. I noted in my diary:

> *The country I flew over today was totally desolate and looked like something from hell, or perhaps to be kinder, the landscape of the moon.*

The major difference between yesterday's 5.9 hour flight and today's 5 hour flight was that I was near the coast, and although I had to contend with a heavy haze and dust, I felt it was not as challenging as the totally desolate and uninhabited environment I found myself in yesterday.

I landed at Gwadar at 5.00pm, and a heavy police presence was immediately evident at this remote little airport. It is situated 5NM due north of the port of Gwadar. The airport manager advised me that Avgas was not available and that I might have to go back to Pasni – about 50NM in the wrong direction. Light aircraft, apparently, rarely flew through Gwadar, and hence only jet fuel was available for the larger commercial aircraft. Every mile gained on my journey was so important to me and I was reluctant to back-track unless I had no alternative. And so I settled for Mogas and four Air Pakistan ground staff, who had just finished work for the day, agreed to drive me into town to organise some. My first impression of Gwadar was that it was a very poor, almost primitive town, with donkey-drawn carts in the main street and a generally low standard of buildings and roads.

The port of Gwadar is on the Makran coast of Baluchistan, the largest province of Pakistan, and lies 260NM west of Karachi. It faces the Arabian Sea and is situated near the head of the Persian Gulf. It is an important port for Pakistan given the significant mineral, oil and natural gas deposits in Baluchistan.

Driving through the town, I noticed two or three petrol

stations, but there was not a petrol pump in sight. They had all been removed as a result of the businesses closing, which I was told was for political reasons – problems with the Irani government who had previously supplied fuel, but who had now cut off their supply completely. The petrol station we finally pulled into had a vacant concrete plinth at the front where two bowsers once stood, but fortunately, the proprietor had two 44-gallon drums of petrol stashed in a shed out the back. I couldn't believe my luck, but got a bit of a shock when I saw them in a dingy, dusty shed – two old, battered and grubby 44-gallon drums, their age and the quality of the fuel in them being anyone's guess. I asked to see a sample in a glass jar and from the colour, clarity and smell, it appeared fine. I picked what I considered was the best of the two drums and my companions promised to have it at the airport by 6.00am the following morning.

Before I left, the proprietor invited me to have a cup of tea with him in the petrol station. It was sweet, black tea once again, but refreshing in the hot, humid conditions. Since this wasn't a tourist town, and Europeans were seldom seen, people kept coming up and looking through the glassless window space to see the strange white man in a flying suit sweating profusely.

On the way to the motel I was taken to the Assistant Commissioner's home so that he could meet me – it was apparently he who would arrange my immigration and landing clearances.

I finally arrived at the Gwadar Tourist Motel, the only one in Gwadar, and it was a dump. It was about a hundred metres from the shoreline and protected by small sand dunes. My room was supposed to be the best in the tiny complex – the "executive room" – but had flapping flywire mesh on the windows and was in a very dirty state. There were two places I could sleep – either on a large, dark-red, Persian style carpet on the floor with several round, bolster type pillows scattered about plus a couple of candle holders, or else the double bed, which hadn't been made since the last person slept in it. The sheets couldn't have been washed in six months.

But for now, I just wanted to get some food into my stomach as I was very hungry. I placed my order for deep fried chicken and rice at a kind of outdoor dining area, and sat and waited. After an hour-and-a-half it still hadn't arrived, despite my being assured three or four times it was only a few minutes away. It wasn't as though they were busy either, with only five or six people at other tables.

When I had been dropped off at the motel earlier, one of the Air Pakistan staff in the car said he would come back and see me later on. Just when I was about to lose all patience with the kitchen staff, this slight Pakistani figure dressed in traditional white flowing garb turned up. He immediately put things right on the food side of things, though instead of deep fried chicken and rice, it was now going to be fish kebabs and rice. My friend told me that while I waited, he would go and get some whisky for us both, which was really the last thing I felt like, and besides, alcohol is forbidden in Pakistan and severe penalties are applied.

By now it was totally dark and I was seated on my own in a detached, dimly lit patio which overlooked the Arabian Sea, not that you could see anything of it. The night was hot and balmy and the only real sensations to me were the warm, gentle breeze on my face and the muffled, melodic sound of waves breaking on the shore. Under normal circumstances, this might have been quite pleasant, even romantic, but I was beginning to feel somewhat edgy and uncomfortable.

My dinner finally arrived, by now two hours late, and it was chicken and rice after all! My friend returned carrying a white plastic bag concealing a large bottle of Johnnie Walker Black Label whisky. Not being a spirits drinker, I agreed to have just a half measure to be sociable while my friend had two or three. All of a sudden, a young boy of around nine or ten came running up the sand pathway to our patio saying that the police were here to see me and to come. My friend immediately put the whisky bottle back in the bag and hid it beside a low wall before proceeding down the path ahead of me to speak to the policeman first. My heart was racing and what was even more disturbing, was that my dinner companion was not only badly slurring his words, but was unable to walk a straight line – he was staggering. I thought – "this is it, he is going to give himself away immediately and I'm going to be caught up in it also."

To my great relief, my friend seemed to know the policeman, whom I'm sure would have detected the smell of whisky on his breath and noted his demeanour. The policeman now wanted to talk to me and I just hoped he wouldn't smell anything on my breath. He checked my passport and then started to ask a few questions about the purpose of my being in Gwadar, where I had come from, my next stop and so on. I was feeling most uncomfortable and went on the defensive saying that could I please now be left alone so that I could look over my plans and get an early night ready for tomorrow. He sensed my agitation and quietly and firmly said, "Look, I am doing this for your own safety." Two armed guards were stationed at the front of the motel all night, and I sometimes wonder if I may have been considered a target for robbery at the motel and also, did my friend, perhaps, have sinister intentions?

I chose the double bed, as filthy as it was, and the staff kindly brought in an electric fan for me. The heat was incredible and my clothes were saturated with perspiration. The fan was very large on a tall metal stand – the type you see in department stores that you can feel the breeze from metres away. The problem with this one was that it only had two speeds: low, which wouldn't blow a feather, and high, which was akin to a hurricane. I settled for the latter.

My diary entry reads:

*Last night would have to go down as my worst ever in trying to sleep. I was a bath of perspiration all night and I don't know how many people had done the same on the same sheets before me. Got up a couple of times to drink water and was glad when it was morning. I showered every morning usually, but on this occasion let it go on account of the filthy bathroom. Couldn't go without my food though, and the guys from the motel made an omelette, tea and toast – not bad at all.*

I arrived at the airport right on 6.30am and the fuel arrived soon after in the back of a utility. It was now in several different metal and plastic containers and they reckoned there was 170 litres.

Soon after transferring the fuel to *Margery*, the Airport Manager arrived to proudly announce that Pakistan had detonated five atomic devices yesterday, more than likely when I was en route from Karachi. In response to my question of, "How far away?" I noted the answer in my diary:

*Apparently only 200 km away from Gwadar – I'm just waiting for the skin to peel off my face and arms.*

With assistance from the Airport Manager in having my flight plan approved, I took off for Dubai at 8.00am, just before a commercial flight was due. Although the weather was generally fine, I encountered considerable haze about two hours out of Dubai and experienced a loss of horizon over the Gulf of Oman for about forty-five minutes – once more I had to concentrate hard on the instruments. With the exception of the final half hour run into Dubai, the remainder of this 6.1 hour leg was entirely over water.

Also, just on 75 percent of this leg was within Iranian territory, and I was repeatedly asked to relay my position and intentions as I traversed the military airspace surrounding Chah

Bahar near the town of Konarak. The air traffic controller seemed to have difficulty in understanding me, and it was with great relief that I left their airspace after thirty minutes without incident.

As I approached the head of the Gulf of Oman the VOR (Visual Omni Reference) part of my GPS, which indicated whether or not I was on track, dropped out for the first time. I put it down to US military intervention, as they had control over the satellites through which the GPS functioned and the system was apparently turned off at random for varying periods of time. I also noted a large amount of shipping in these parts, which might have had something to do with it. With the adjoining Persian Gulf just to the north, it was a militarily sensitive region.

At 85NM, I made contact with a passing commercial airliner on frequency 121.5 and the captain relayed my position and ETA to Dubai Control. Upon leaving the Gulf, just south of the coastal town of Khawr Fakkan, I had to climb to 4,000 feet to pass over a rugged and desolate mountain range before descending to 2,000 feet over an equally barren, sandy landscape. This final thirty minutes of the flight was hot and bumpy, and the haze was so severe on approach to Dubai, I found it difficult to sight the airport.

As I descended to the runway on finals, the wind continued strong and gusty and the tower informed me it was 15 knots and 20° off the nose. I was happy with my landing under such awkward conditions and taxied up to park next to the guys in the seaplane I had met in Karachi. I was hot and tired and after being confined to the cockpit for most of the day, I couldn't wait to get out and stretch my legs. My backside was also aching badly and I knew I had to do something urgently with my seating arrangement to try and relieve it. As I was tying down *Margery* for the night, an American air traffic controller, who had been on duty at the time of my landing, came down to meet me and made me feel very welcome.

When I entered the air terminal I was given a handwritten note, signed Evelyn Brey, secretary of the Dubai Flying Club, who said she would like to meet me and could I please give her a call. By the time I reached the hotel, I was exhausted and dehydrated. A cool shower and a couple of glasses of water soon revived me. I then called Evelyn who met me in the foyer where cold drinks were served, and we spent the next twenty minutes or so exchanging stories. She was small in stature, in her early thirties and impressed me with her friendly manner and smile. The Meridian Hotel was a palace compared to the motel in Gwadar, and I was really looking forward to a day off. Before crashing into bed, I rang home and managed to speak to three of my four children (unfortunately Brad was working) and granddaughter, Gabrielle. It was so uplifting.

The following morning I slept in until 7.00am and ate a hearty breakfast. I then went to the airport to pick up the replacement tacho cable April had sent from Perth, and to see if there was someone to help fit it. Evelyn was also there, and she introduced me to Raj, a Sri Lankan, who was the Dubai Flying Club's engineer.

Raj, his two helpers and myself set about finding the best way to replace the cable without removing the long-range tank in the front cockpit. It looked impossible, until I suggested that we pull out the inner broken cable, leaving the casing, and then thread through a piece of wire to pull through the new inner cable. It worked! Being the first to acknowledge my distinct lack of natural ability concerning motors, and engineering in general, I tried not to get a swollen head out of this, but I couldn't help feeling some satisfaction at having come up with this suggestion.

Apart from a few short breaks, we spent five hours standing in the sun rectifying the cable problem and the ground temperature was at least 50°C. I drank copious amounts of water and felt as if I was about to melt. I was amazed that Raj, a much older man with a wiry frame and greying hair, was not affected as much as me – he was obviously accustomed to these conditions. And although it was my idea to thread the wire, it still proved to be a most difficult task, and it was only Raj's doggedness and determination to complete the job that finally made it succeed, whilst my physical strength and concentration were fading fast. In fact, when standing on top of the engine cowl to refuel *Margery* later in the day, I felt faint and nearly fell off.

Although I was keen to push on, my body was telling me I needed a break, and so I decided to stay an extra day and forego the next scheduled rest day in Bahrain. It would also give me a chance to fix the leaking rocker hats (tappet covers).

During the day, I had a brief conversation with the CFI (Chief Flying Instructor) and he impressed upon me the dangers of dust and haze in the region. I sensed he was concerned how I would handle these conditions, and he certainly didn't instil any confidence in me. Once again, I started to feel sick in the stomach as I contemplated what I might be facing over the next few days. The worst thing was being stuck on the ground with my fears, and I knew in my heart that the only remedy was to become airborne again and get on with it – but, that would have to wait a day.

That evening, Evelyn invited me for drinks at the Boardwalk Café in the Dubai Creek Yacht Club. We sat outside overlooking the inlet or "The Creek", as locals refer to it, and had an interesting discussion on a variety of topics including life in Dubai, family, and of course our common interest, flying.

From there we progressed to dinner at the Nad Al Shiba Club. It is a prestigious, well appointed race track and golf club complex, and is popular with international celebrities. I felt slightly underdressed and uncomfortable wearing the best of my very limited clothing, and the fact that I had just extracted it from the bottom of my duffel bag. Arriving at the Club after dark, one of the first things I noticed were the bright lights of the fully floodlit, eighteen-hole golf course. The adjoining Nad Al Shiba race track hosts the world's richest annual horse race with the purse, reportedly, at six million dollars (US).

But although the meal and surrounds were excellent, I couldn't totally relax, thinking of what lay ahead of me – particularly the Saudi Arabian desert.

Dubai had a clean, modern feel to it with high-rise apartments, office buildings and hotels dominating the city skyline. There were also souqs, or markets, and it was at one of these that I replaced some of my lost clothing. The additional rest day also gave me the chance to go over my charts carefully and have a haircut.

Arriving at the airport next morning, I found poor *Margery* covered in dust. Fortunately the cockpit cover had been on, but the dust had got through the air intake on the nose cowl and into the engine bay. She was now looking like a real work-horse, but cleaning her would have to wait for another day – I had to push on.

Of the Dubai to Bahrain leg, I later wrote in my diary:

> *Today's flight of 5.3 hours was just about all over water*
> *– The Persian Gulf. Although there was no weather as*
> *such, the visibility was generally poor on account of the*
> *haze and there was no horizon after about 1½ hours.*
> *Very demanding flying and was on instruments (with just*
> *a glance down to the water every now and again) for*
> *most of the time. My backside was aching badly (again)*
> *and I found it difficult to make myself comfortable. Two*
> *aircraft (commercial airliners) helped me with position*
> *reports and this was greatly appreciated. A number of*
> *aircraft were coming into Bahrain at the same time, and*
> *as I was the slowest by far, I had to hold out over the Gulf*
> *for some 20 minutes – it was quite pleasant actually, as*
> *the runway was visible from some 12NM out, so I didn't*
> *feel under any pressure. Landing could have been better,*
> *but I put it down to feeling very tired and not entirely*
> *well.*

The airport is on a small island named Muharraq. Approaching the island, I could see the City of Bahrain far in the distance to my left on the mainland. From the air, the airport and runway dominated the island; there was no sign of vegetation. Although the runway stood out, a fair amount of haze was present and the whole island had a brown-grey appearance.

The Dubai to Bahrain leg was really hard slog, and at about the halfway mark, I said to myself – "I shouldn't be up here." As I had done in India, I resorted to folding the doors down and tried to lift myself on outstretched elbows to relieve the pain in my posterior. But inhaling the sickening fuel fumes rising from the cockpit floor, as a result of a leaking wobble pump, and feeling generally debilitated, it was a real struggle.

As I was tying *Margery* down, two smartly dressed Aussie pilots came over to look at *Margery* and have a bit of a chat. Although only in their early twenties, they were in command of a light twin owned by Falcon Express, and were clearly enjoying themselves.

For a welcome change, I didn't have to worry about customs and immigration procedures as I was staying at the Transotel Hotel which was within the airport precinct. This meant I couldn't leave the airport, but I didn't mind at all. After a shower and a meal of soup and shish kebabs, I was a new man again. With the light now fading, I sat against the window of the near empty visitors lounge and watched a number of aircraft come and go. Far over to my left, I could just make out *Margery* tied down, with red cockpit cover on, ready for her well deserved night's rest. Once I had checked over my plans for tomorrow, I too would be having an early night. Before anything though, I rang home and the inner peace I felt after talking to my family, as on every other occasion, was amazing – I could actually feel the built-up strain and tension draining from my body.

# Chapter 9

# BAHRAIN TO JEDDAH

**Days 38-46** - 2 June 1998 to 10 June 1998

Since leaving home, one of my most feared sections was crossing the expansive desert of the Arabian peninsula: now the day of reckoning had arrived. Departing Bahrain, I was almost immediately over the Persian Gulf again, but not for long this time. Even through the light haze, the water was surprisingly clear with very little surface disturbance and I could clearly make out the beige tones of several underwater reef and rock formations.

I was now at my cruising altitude of 4,500 feet, and after being radar vectored around the controlled airspace of Dhahran, was on my own and heading straight into the desert. Excitement overcame fear as I marvelled at the extent of the yellow-brown sand landscape that stretched in all directions as far as the eye could see.

This sense of excitement was soon jolted, though, by the sight of the red alternator warning light coming on, not just once, but several times. Fortunately, I was able to recycle it each time simply by turning the master switch off then on again. To lose all electrics out here, including my radio and GPS, would have placed me in a very serious predicament, for to navigate accurately over such featureless country is a difficult exercise even at the best of times. Obviously my battery was not being recharged by the alternator at a sufficient rate.

On reaching my IFR reporting point of Almal, an imaginary spot in the desert about the halfway mark to Riyadh, I made the unforgivable mistake of turning on to an incorrect heading. Within a minute, I knew I was flying in the wrong direction, so immediately commenced a couple of gentle left hand orbits to try and sort myself out. In doing so, the GPS went haywire so it was now back to basics, checking and rechecking the required heading from my chart to the flight plan, estimating where I was in relation to the last reporting point – which, fortunately, was within a couple of miles, and then taking up the required heading to get back on track for Riyadh.

The dust was now beginning to build up, and in combination with the haze, affected visibility considerably. I was thankful that I had made an early departure, 6.40am, as strongly advised by the flying instructor in Dubai.

At about 40NM from Riyadh, I made contact with the tower and was surprised to hear an Aussie voice at the other end! He was also surprised to hear my voice. The brief exchange of a sentence or two with a fellow Australian, so far from home, helped put me at ease.

I was placed in front of an inbound commercial airliner and told to call on finals, Runway 15. Exactly how far out the airliner was I didn't know, and although feeling anxious about being number 1, followed instructions. To my utter amazement, when I was on short finals the tower told the airliner to carry out a 360° turn. The captain wasn't very happy about it and told the tower he should have had priority as there were "122 souls on board". Apparently no one was aware of the snail-like performance of a Tiger Moth.

It was now around 11.00am and in the hot, buffeting conditions it was difficult to hold *Margery* steady when rounding out to land. After a few tense moments, I was finally able to plant the main wheels, then holding the stick forward and into wind, I waited to feel the increased back pressure in my hand before allowing *Margery's* tail to drop gently to the ground.

The taxi was my longest, anywhere – a full twenty minutes which included crossing a bridge to the General Aviation apron.

Feeling hot and tired in my sweat-saturated flying suit, which was stuck to me like plastic cling-wrap, I dropped my bags on a small table in front of a customs officer, half expecting to be ushered straight through. But not today. He proceeded to go through my limited luggage and then, out of my canvas army duffel bag, pulled out one, two and finally three cans of Fosters lager. The eyes of this previously sullen, expressionless man now took on an evil glint as he lined the cans up and summoned his colleagues over to inspect the contraband. From the excitement in their voices, they were obviously enjoying the moment. I felt ill and inwardly castigated myself for being so stupid as to bring a prohibited substance, such as alcohol, into a country like Saudi Arabia. In all honesty, I hadn't even thought about it. I'd wanted to purchase just one can of beer at Bahrain Airport, but was only able to buy a six pack. I drank one, left two in my hotel room, and decided to bring the remaining three with me.

While the customs officers went off in a huddle to discuss my fate, I was told to stay put. After twenty minutes, the officer returned saying that I was to pay an on-the-spot fine of US$66.00. I objected strongly, saying that I felt it was a minor breach and I needed every dollar I had to pay for fuel to reach England. After some forty-five minutes of argument, the officer finally relented and I was ordered to follow him into the men's toilets to witness the cans being emptied down the drain.

As the last can was opened, the officer turned to me with a smirk on his face and said, "Like some?" I shook my head. With great delight he held the can high and let it slowly pour out. I could have cheerfully throttled him there and then, not on account of the lost beer, but because of his sheer arrogance.

It hadn't been the smoothest of days and I wrote in my diary:

> *My backside is extremely sore now and I'm not in any condition to fly tomorrow. Might have to see a doctor/ change seat cushioning, etc. Also, they have to get some Avgas in for me which won't come until 10.00am. The pilots of a privately owned Boeing 727 whom I met today (an Englishman and an American) told me that to avoid the dust storms, I should take off around 5.30am – another reason I'll stay here an extra day. My first impression of Saudi Arabia isn't very good and even one of the locals told me that the country, as a whole, is over restricted and controlled.*

On ringing home, I was told that our thirteen-year-old black Labrador, Samson, had passed away. My diary entry continued:

> *Was really saddened to hear that poor old Sam was put down today – I shed a quiet tear – I will not be taking my old mate for a walk any more. Feeling very tired and a bit down tonight – just want to reach England.*

The following morning after breakfast, I went straight to the local hospital to try to get something to relieve my ever-present pain. Unfortunately, the doctor seemed most uninterested in my problem, and didn't even examine me – not that I particularly wanted him to – and sent me away after a few minutes consultation with just four anti-inflammatory tablets. The Avgas was ordered in especially for me and a small, old, dark-green Mercedes tanker arrived at the gate just after 10.00am. And there it sat, with its nose against the steel bars of the gate for the next four-and-a-half hours: what the problem was nobody would say, but I was relieved to finally fill *Margery*'s tanks, sufficient for the long trip to Jeddah.

While waiting, I sat in the air-conditioned ground handler's office (outside, it was around 50°C) and spoke to a number of commercial pilots who were coming and going. One American pilot who had just pulled up in a Gulfstream jet, called over the radio, "Who owns the Gipsy Moth?" After talking back to him over the radio for a short time, explaining it was actually a Tiger Moth, and where I was heading, he said, "I'll buy you a pint – but not in Saudi."

The only chores I carried out were to tape up the number 1 spark plug lead and recharge the battery. Late in the day, I was hit with a bill for US$1,045 for ground handling and landing charges. The excuse proffered by the ground handlers for this exorbitant fee, was that the Saudi authorities did not distinguish between a Boeing 747 and a Tiger Moth – everyone paid the same fee.

Returning to the hotel, I was pleasantly surprised to receive phone calls from two hard-working members of my support team, Gerry Gannon and John Roberts, back in Perth. This was followed by a call from my sister, June, and her husband, John. As family members, their continued support and encouragement meant a lot. I was in bed by 9.00pm to be ready for an early rise to fly my longest leg yet – 462NM.

I never got used to the beep-beep-beep wake-up alarm on my watch and the morning of 4 June (Day 40) was no exception when it went off at 3.45am. It always sent a small shiver through me. In simple terms, it was an order for me to leave the security of my warm and comfortable bed, climb into my flying suit and face the music – whatever that might be.

Because of my preparations the previous day, I was airborne by 5.50am. Turning crosswind, I looked back over my left shoulder to say goodbye to Riyadh. Already the runways and airport buildings were beginning to blend into the yellow-brown landscape. By mid morning, I could almost feel the earth heating up beneath me and my cruising altitude of 4,500 feet was becoming unbearable on account of the turbulence and the constant buffeting I was receiving. So I climbed to 6,500 feet which helped a little.

Below me was the Saudi Arabian Desert, which covers the entire peninsula. I was fascinated by its vastness and stark beauty. I saw a lot of wildlife, including many herds of camels and what I thought were horses. I also saw several small nomadic settlements, or camps, surrounded by desert sand and with no visible vegetation. It was amazing that people could survive in such conditions, but it was something they had done for centuries. Whenever I saw one of these camps, about every hour or so, my eyes remained glued to it until it disappeared from sight – for I saw it as a lifeline if I happened to be forced down in this most inhospitable country. In the case of engine failure, or perhaps a dust storm, I would try and land as close as possible to one of the camps.

The alternator warning light started coming on after about two hours, and although I managed to recycle it a few times, finally it just stayed on, meaning that the battery was not being recharged by the alternator. After about five hours, I noticed an interesting change in the landscape, which went from yellow-brown sand to black rock. It was solidified lava, and looking directly down, I could see the beautiful swirling, paisley-like patterns which had been created by the lava flow just prior to it setting.

At 60NM from Jeddah, I had to climb to 7,000 feet to cross a rocky, barren mountain range. As I commenced the climb from the east, I encountered strong headwinds and turbulence, and it seemed to take forever to reach the top and then commence my descent on the other side. Since it was one o'clock in the afternoon, with the ground at its maximum temperature, it was little wonder I experienced a rough ride. At 50NM inbound, I decided to try and make contact with Jeddah control and turned my transponder on only to find that the annunciator light was very dim. A now familiar sinking feeling came over me as I realised I would, in all probability, lose all electrics, including the GPS and radio, before I reached Jeddah. Nevertheless, I broadcast my intentions and proceeded in.

It was at about this point that I noticed a spectacular crater formation with a flattened white rim, surrounded by solidified black lava. At first I thought it was a meteor crash site, but a local in Jeddah later told me that it was the weathered rim of an old volcano. Within a few minutes, I was abeam the Mecca control zone just 18NM to the south, and I had been given stern warnings in Riyadh not to contravene their air space under any circumstances. Maintaining accurate use of the compass and careful timekeeping were essential, for the electrics, and with it the radio and GPS, could fail at any time and if they did, I needed to know precisely where I was on the map, and more importantly, to know that I was clear of Mecca.

The tension was really building up now, and just when I thought I had about fifteen minutes to run, I was vectored away from the airport by a good 20NM to 30NM to allow a couple of commercial airliners and 'Air Force One' to complete their approaches and land. At 15NM my radio began to fail, so I requested the tower to allow me in without delay. The controller told me I could proceed in and to expect to join base, runway 34 right. But at 15NM, in hazy conditions, the airport was nowhere in sight. I continued on my assigned heading, and then at 11NM the radio screen went black – I had lost everything. At that precise moment, I just managed to see the faint outline of the airport. Rather than on base, I was on very long finals and very worried about other traffic – especially big jets that might be around.

I fumbled to connect my reserve hand-held radio and GPS, only to find it was unusable on account of static noise, and I had no time to play around with it. So I broadcast my intentions anyway and proceeded in.

Coming down on finals, it was as if my head was on a swivel, and I was in a cold sweat just hoping like hell that I would not get an aircraft up the back of me. I don't know how, but the landing was great. Just before departing the runway, I could see over to my right a long line of camouflage-painted C-130 Hercules aircraft which, I later found out were part of a British squadron. Just looking at the sheer size of these, I was glad that they were all parked when I was coming in. Over the next few days, I frequently saw them taking off and landing like big graceful birds.

I parked just off the runway with the engine still running, waiting for someone to come along and give me directions, but no one did. I spotted two Arabs sitting in, what appeared to be, an airport station wagon about sixty metres away, so I taxied over and hailed them to come and show me the way. I was certain that all hell would break loose because of the radio failure, but not a single question was asked. The flight had taken eight-and-a-quarter hours and it took a little effort to extract myself from the tight confines of the cockpit. After twenty minutes or so of walking around, a proper blood supply returned to my extremities, particularly my legs, and I started to feel normal once more.

Since the following day was Friday, the Islamic holy day, I was able to sleep in a little, knowing that the aircraft maintenance facilities would be closed. Later in the day, I rang friends of my neighbours, Will and Ingrid Reeder, who were living in Jeddah. Will was a medical practitioner employed by a local tractor and heavy machinery company.

With evening approaching, Will picked me up from my hotel and took me on a wonderful sightseeing trip of the city which took in the Corniche, a long seaside boulevard, the souq (market) and Obhur Creek, with jet skis racing up and down. There were numerous large statues along the Corniche that seemed to have religious significance, and other works of art including a great water spout and the famous Jars. The various works of art were, apparently, donated by large companies. The Jars were situated in an area known as Alhambra, described as being part of the old uptown of Jeddah and near Salam Palace. They consisted of four huge, colourful jars, or vase shapes, positioned in a line, each suspended from a steel tripod frame and standing approximately 40 feet high. A local man explained that jars were traditionally a symbol of giving or providing, based on the premise that they contained wealth, and this is what he believed the artwork represented. He described The Jars as being a middle-eastern version of Feng Shui.

Small groups of men dressed in traditional thobes (white cotton robes) could be seen sitting cross-legged on the wide concrete pavement of the Corniche adjoining the Obhur Creek, peacefully whiling away the time. In another section, children were taking donkey rides. The souq was crowded and bustling, and a happy mood prevailed on this clear, warm night as the stall-holders plied their trade and customers looked for bargains. Spice stalls were popular, as were the leather stalls selling Arabic sandals. A forlorn-looking camel was tethered to a pole outside one of the larger buildings. For dinner we had a typical souq meal of shewarma (Arabic bread rolled about chicken and spices) and orange juice.

Before returning me to my hotel, Will took me home to meet his family. He also investigated my backside problem, and the official diagnosis was ischial bursitis, or an inflammation of the membrane covering the base of the pelvis. He gave me some anti-inflammatory tablets and recommended I sit on a doughnut cushion when flying from now on – a car tyre tube would be perfect if I could get hold of one. Without another word being said, Ingrid took a loose cushion from the couch and disappeared into her sewing room to return, about twenty minutes later, with her own-design doughnut cushion. She had simply cut the centre out and then sewed around the opening. I was touched by her kindness and thoughtfulness.

The next five days were the most frustrating of my entire trip, as I tried to have my electrical problem fixed. The alternator was removed and replaced three times. The work was so poor, that after the second attempt to fix the problem had failed, it was found that the new electrical brushes had fallen out and were sitting in the bottom of the case. To add to my frustration, my visa was valid for only twenty-four hours, and I had to go through the process of renewing it each morning. In granting me this temporary visa, I was told that I was only permitted to travel between my hotel and the airport. Obviously I had bent the rules with my sightseeing tour on the second day and, for my part, there was a slightly rebellious sense of satisfaction in having done so.

But spending so many hours at the airport, I met a number of commercial pilots and was delighted to be shown over some of the most expensive and beautifully appointed aircraft I'd ever seen. An American pilot of one of the Princes of Saudi Arabia's personal aircraft, a Boeing 707, said that the fit-out carried out in Texas eight years earlier had cost over forty million dollars. It was absolutely luxurious and included a bedroom and en suite with gold plated taps. Other luxuriously appointed aircraft included a Boeing 727, a DC8 and a brand new Falcon 900. The Falcon was flown by a Swiss pilot, who allowed me some time to day-dream in the captain's seat. A 1956 twin-engined Convair also operated out of Jeddah, and its two American crew kindly showed me through it and were obviously attached to their big, characterful workhorse.

Fauzi, a young man who worked for Jet Aviation ground-handlers, must have sensed my frustration and went out of his way to assist me in whatever way he could. He even located and fixed my fuel leak problem which turned out to be a worn O-ring in the wobble pump.

One day, the wind got up to 25 knots, and the other side of the airfield was barely visible through the dust. I wondered what affect it had on the jet engines of arriving and departing aircraft and was momentarily glad that *Margery* was grounded.

Another day, while I was killing time in the empty airport lounge, a high-ranking USAF officer came in and was met by two generals. Being only a few feet away, I overheard that they had just completed an inspection of all US military bases in the Middle East, with Jeddah being the last. Two of the officers were wearing Desert Storm camouflage gear and the other was dressed in a dark-green Marines' uniform. Parked directly out the front, was their USAF-marked light twin aircraft.

Although I was still well within log book limits, while the technicians worked on the electrics, I took advantage of the available time to carry out an oil change and readjust the tappets. My sense of frustration and disappointment at being stuck in Jeddah is evident in my diary entry of 8 June 1998 – the fourth day:

> *They (the technicians) spent all day on it and we finally had an engine run at 7.00pm. Alternator light was still staying on! No one could believe it, after all that effort with 2-3 guys working on it all day the problem still exists. I have now gone past the point of being exasperated and simply accept that there is a problem in hand which must be fixed one way or the other before I can depart for Luxor. Poor Fauzi seemed totally exhausted (as with the rest of us) when we finally gave it away at about 8.15pm. My feet are really aching from standing on the hard concrete for a good part of the day.*

Hoping to be able to depart within the next day or two,

I carefully went over my charts and flight plans. John Roberts had also been doing some homework, and sent me a fax suggesting I shorten my Red Sea crossing (which, as it stood, was quite a long diagonal) by travelling further north up the eastern coast of the Red Sea before heading west into Egypt. It was a good suggestion, and I followed it, but I had to modify it slightly on the day. Sunny, my secretary back in Perth, also sent up some welcome weather information that indicated I would need to be through the Cairo region in the next three days to avoid a forecast build-up of weather.

On the fifth day, the problem finally appeared to be fixed and I could concentrate on departing next morning. Being in the Aerobasco hangar all day for five days, I had now become used to the twice-daily ritual of the Muslim employees, who would stop work to pay homage to Allah. The prayer session began with the 'leader' chanting over a loud speaker a sung prayer, which was rather monotonous, but haunting. Workers lined up their individual carpet mats on the hangar floor facing Mecca, and then knelt, before placing their foreheads on the ground. Each prayer session took about half an hour and I couldn't get over what an important part religion plays in their daily lives.

After topping up with fuel and lodging my flight plan for the Jeddah-Luxor leg, I was informed that the Saudi authorities were not going to extend my visa for a further twenty-four hours and that I would have to leave Saudi Arabia the next day - with or without *Margery*. If I chose to stay, I would be fined 3,000 riyals per day (about A$1,000). This was adding insult to injury, for I had already been charged huge amounts for landing charges and the electrical 'repairs'. I couldn't wait to leave the country.

I rang Carol in the evening. She was now patiently waiting for me in England. I felt for her, because I was now a fortnight behind schedule.

# Chapter 10

# JEDDAH TO ALEXANDRIA

**Days 47-48** - 11 June 1998 to 12 June 1998

My diary for 11 June commenced:

*Alarm set for 3.50am to ensure I get a good start. A 470NM or approx. 8 hour run. Quick (cup of) tea, cereal, bacon and eggs and then to airport, arriving at around 5.30am – sun still not up. Waited for the inevitable bill and then went and prepared Margery – cover off, check fuel and oil levels, fuel drains (4), turn oil filter, check aeroplane over and load baggage and water and biscuits – very important. Finally started up at 6.20am and what a relief it was to take off. I just hoped and prayed I didn't have to return to Jeddah for any reason. Backside started aching again after no more than an hour – same old thing – wriggle around as best you can, sit on one hand – then the other, etc.*

Captain Tim Forman, an American Raytheon Airline Captain had generously given me an ONC chart covering the west coast of Saudi Arabia adjoining the Red Sea, as this area was just off the edge of the trimmed down chart for my original route.

I would now travel approximately 160NM up the coast before commencing the water crossing, which would add about 40NM, or forty minutes to the leg, though I considered it would be safer as my actual time over the water should be less.

One of the waypoints ahead, Gibal, was an IFR (Instrument Flight Rules) reporting point used by commercial air traffic, and had been included in my flight plan at the instruction of the aviation authorities in Jeddah. It was an imaginary point in the Red Sea.

Although visibility was good, I had a headwind most of the way, and in the first two or three hours, my ground speed was only 55 knots. I began to worry about my fuel reserves, and rather than continue to Yenbo, decided to cut the corner and head straight across the Red Sea. This anxiety was largely self-induced for I had made the decision, when refuelling in Jeddah, not to fill the tanks to capacity in order to save weight, confident that I would comfortably make the distance in under nine hours. I didn't make this mistake again. As the saying goes, "There's no benefit in empty tank space." Ninety minutes later, I estimated I was at Gibal, and became even more alarmed when after some mental calculations, realised at my current rate of travel, at best I might just reach Luxor with no reserves, and at worst, would be landing in the desert about 30NM short of Luxor.

Panic mounted as I visualised landing in a remote part of the desert. *Margery* was starting to wander around the skies a little, I was not holding altitude properly and my throttle was too far advanced, probably a subconscious action to get me there quicker. In short, I was not flying accurately. I chastised myself for this brief moment of poor airmanship and immediately proceeded to do something about it. I reduced the throttle setting from 2,100 RPM to 1,950 RPM, I trimmed *Margery* to my assigned cruising altitude of 4,500 feet and then leaned the mixture slightly. Then I concentrated on my scan – wings-level, needle in the middle (using rudder pedals), altitude steady, selecting the correct heading to maintain my track of 287°, and RPM steady on 1,950 RPM. I made a conscious effort to relax my grip on the controls and, before I knew it, I was flying as accurately and smoothly as I had ever done. I knew that it was important to maintain this standard of flying to conserve fuel.

Flying over the Red Sea, I thought of its significance in Biblical times and of Moses parting the waves to save the fleeing Israelites. It seemed to take forever to reach the Egyptian coast and all the while, my mind was preoccupied with the ever-diminishing fuel supply. One positive sign was that my ground speed had now improved to 65 knots. When I reached the Egyptian coast, at precisely 0841 UTC, the water crossing from east to west had taken a total of 3 hours and 5 minutes. A small mountain range near the coast, with the highest peak around 5,000 feet, was my first obstacle, but within minutes of crossing it, the wind had turned around and I was now achieving a ground speed of 75 to 80 knots. I was over pure desert sands again, but that didn't matter at all – I knew I would now reach Luxor, and with fuel to spare, albeit not a lot.

As I neared Luxor, the irrigated farmlands abutting the Nile River stood out as a brilliant green ribbon stretching north and south as far as the eye could see, bisecting the heavily contrasted yellow-brown desert sands. After a long flight of 7 hours and 20 minutes (470 NM), I was pleased to execute a good landing. As any pilot will testify, there is never anyone to witness the good landings, only the bad ones, but I'm sure some of my Aero Club mates back home would have been proud of this one!

I felt very tired when I finally climbed out of the cockpit and was not really in the mood for the pushy refueller who was pressing me for a gift of money – even before he had put fuel in the tanks. Even so, I felt some sympathy for him and gave him a tip when refuelling was completed. Immigration and customs procedures were easy, particularly after Saudi Arabia, and I made my way to the Sheraton Hotel, right on the Nile River. After checking into my room and having a shower, I set about getting a lift to one of the ancient temple sites, for I knew that with no more scheduled rest days until the Greek island of Corfu, this would be my only opportunity to experience one of the most ancient cultures in the world and see ruins of immense archaeological importance. The Temple of Karnak was magnificent and I couldn't believe that I was standing within these ancient Egyptian ruins, thousands of years old.

By the time I arrived back at the Sheraton, it was late afternoon. The air was warm and dry, and I sat out on the Hotel concourse with a cold drink. It was a beautiful sight with date palms, lush green grass and plants in the foreground, small motor boats and sail boats gliding slowly down the river, and then the soft yellow-red glow of the sun on the high, barren mountains in the background where the Queen Hatshepsut Temple, Valley of the Kings and Valley of the Queens are situated. The sun slipped from view and night descended. Behind me a small group of men were otherwise absorbed, watching World Cup soccer on television (being played in France) while smoking their hookah pipes. Although it was only part of one day in Egypt, it was such a richly satisfying moment that I knew I would never forget it.

The following morning I was up at 6.00am, though I didn't get firing as early as usual, perhaps because at 374NM, this was a significantly shorter leg than the previous two, and hence there was no great urgency to get away. I started up at 8.00am, but had to shut down again as the red alternator light was not indicating at all – it should illuminate for a brief moment and then go straight off again as the alternator starts working. There were two possible problems – either the battery was flat or the alternator was faulty. After experimenting with a few different ideas, I pressed on the face of the radio console with my thumb – near the master switch – only to see the red light suddenly illuminate. Obviously there was a loose wire underneath, but knowing that the odds of getting this problem fixed in Luxor were slim, and having a burning desire to keep going, I restarted *Margery* and departed immediately for Alexandria. I wrote in my diary:

> *Very strong headwind to start with (ground speed varied 50-58 knots) and I thought I was in for a very long haul. With the exception of the Nile, which is a stunning ribbon of green with the river running through the middle, the majority of the trip was over pure desert – I am really thankful I didn't have to put down in it – chances of survival would be a bit slim if weren't found fairly quickly.*

The landscape was extremely hot and dry and I took the precaution of taking regular sips of water. About two hours into the journey, I noticed a strip of gaffer tape starting to peel from the right aileron where it joined the wing. I had originally placed it there, back in Indonesia, following a severe rainstorm which had stripped the paint from the fabric gap seal. Although it was probably not essential to tape it over, it seemed some insurance against the exposed area of fabric being damaged in some way. To date, I had replaced the tape twice. Inch by inch, the approximately four-foot length of tape slowly peeled from the wing until there was a three-foot long streamer trailing behind. It kept me amused for a considerable time as I tried to guess when it would fall away, but at the same time I was hoping that there wasn't a weak area in the exposed section that might tear with the force of the wind. It finally parted company with *Margery* on descent into Alexandria.

Although not landing at Cairo Airport, I was within the 20NM Control Zone, and for the next thirty minutes or so came under the direction of the radar controller. I was now travelling up the east bank of the Nile, and at around 15NM passed directly over Hulwan Airport, its solitary runway clearly visible. Looking out to my left, just a few miles further on, I sighted my first pyramid at Dashur, some 5-6NM away. It was in the desert, just beyond the green belt of the Nile. Continuing northwards, and once again looking out to my left, a cluster of three pyramids came into view. They were the pyramids of Giza named Cheops, Chephren and Mycerinus. I was excited to see these ancient world-wonders and kept craning my neck for a final glimpse, for I knew I would be unlikely to ever have this view again.

My radar-directed track next took us over Old Cairo (Misr Al-Qadima) and Ar-Rauda Island, with its multitude of grey-brown buildings and Cairo University Hospital at the northern tip. At the southern end of Ar-Rauda Island, the Al-Giza Bridge, and smaller Al-Malik Bridge (which connect the western and eastern sides of the island with the mainland) stood out against the darker blue-green colour of the Nile.

As I crossed the Nile, the Zoological Gardens and huge Cairo University campus came into view. My track had taken me away from the central business district of Cairo which lay a couple of miles to the north-east, on the eastern side of the river. With a population of over fifteen million, Cairo is the largest city in Africa as well as the Middle East.

Cairo Airport was very busy and the radar controller had a hint of nervousness in his voice as he worked hard to guide this slow, antiquated flying machine of mine through the maze.I was directed just to the left of the airport and, at one point, was surprised to see a large jet, in the climb, pass from right to left – seemingly not that far above my flight path. The radar controller was directing me closely at this point, and I imagined there were sighs of relief all round when I departed the area.

A strong crosswind and wind gusts resulted in an awkward though safe landing at Alexandria. A further factor might have been the large scrub fire with black, billowing smoke near finals that the tower controller had warned me about when I was 5NM out. My aching backside problem had also returned on this leg, as the doughnut cushion, with my constant weight on it, was now no more than a flattened ring. The pain was almost unbearable, and remembering the advice of Dr Will Reeder in Jeddah, I stopped by a tyre shop on my way to the hotel and purchased an inner tube. It was small in size (145-10) to ensure it fitted into the cockpit and the shop owner inflated it for me. I needed a cover for it though, and in my hotel room found the perfect solution – a pillow case. I felt somewhat guilty taking it, but weakly rationalised that, surely, my room tariff would adequately cover an item as insignificant as a pillow case. Anyway, it was decidedly more comfortable as I later sat on it, in my room, to write my daily diary entry:

> *Had dinner around 7.00pm and then went for a walk along the beach front. It is a warm balmy evening. Today was around 45°C in Alexandria, so the beach is absolutely packed with people, for I would say, at least 3km. Literally thousands of people standing ankle to waist deep in the calm water. Numerous high-rise hotels and apartments look out over the sea. Buildings, however, appear to be of very poor quality and the area is not particularly clean.*
>
> *But, I have a good feeling for the place, the people are very friendly and basically just seem to enjoy themselves. Men smoking hookah pipes in little street-side cafés, food vendors on the beach, kites flying, lots of families and traffic – a bit of a fun atmosphere.*

It was a beautiful, colourful, vibrant sight, with the golden rays of the setting sun shining on the water, people, kites and buildings behind. Earlier in the afternoon I had stood out on the small side balcony of my hotel room, which looked directly out over the Mediterranean Sea in roughly the direction I would be travelling tomorrow. This was a long over-water crossing that I expected would take between five and six hours, depending on the wind. I was disturbed at the sight of a thick sea haze, which, from experience, I knew would be a challenge because of the probable loss of horizon.

Back in my hotel after my evening walk, I looked over my plans once more for tomorrow and remembered the sea haze I had seen earlier. From the northern coast of Africa to the coast of Crete is around 300NM, with not even the hint of an island in between. This was daunting to think of, and I started recalling some of the dangers I had been through up to now and how fortunate I had been to come through unscathed. That triggered a few morbid thoughts. I started to think of Carol waiting for me in England, and how patient she had been. On the one hand I was so close, yet on the other it was still so far away, for there were some difficult water crossings and terrain to cover. I momentarily went weak at the knees, thinking, "What if something should happen to me now? What if I don't make it?" These thoughts and feelings weren't so much for myself, but for Carol.

But, as in Singapore, when similar negative thoughts had started to surface, they were quickly dispelled from my mind and replaced, instead, with positive ones. I went to sleep happy, thinking that if I concentrated hard, flew accurately and there were no unforeseen problems, such as bad weather or breakdowns, God willing, I would soon be reunited with my family and friends.

# Chapter 11

# ALEXANDRIA TO CORFU

**Days 49-53** - 13 June 1998 to 17 June 1998

ocking myself out my room for a quarter of an hour this morning, wearing nothing but my boxer shorts, seemed to set the pattern for the day ahead. I had awoken to my  watch alarm at 5.00am and my pre-ordered breakfast arrived ten minutes later. Breakfast was important today, as I wanted to be sure I was adequately nourished for what I believed could be a demanding flight. As with all previous days of the trip, the night before I had tried to plan, as best I could, every minute – from getting up, having breakfast, travelling to the airport, obtaining a weather report, lodging my flight plan, obtaining customs and immigration clearances, pre-flighting *Margery* and then taking off.

However, just as the hotel porter had shut the door behind him, I noticed there was no toast – most important for breakfast, I thought. And so, dressed just in my boxer shorts, I went racing out into the lobby area of the third floor to tell him. I had barely taken two steps when the door went bang! Horror, I was locked out of my room. The porter was nowhere to be seen and I tracked the elevator lights downwards – second, first, ground floor. Within an instant, my slick start to the day was in disarray. In reality, the situation wasn't bad at all, it's just that I was living on a knife edge – concerned about the long over-water flight ahead of me, and was perceiving a minor annoyance as something major.

Undaunted, I recalled the lift to the third floor and then went down to the ground floor still only in my boxer shorts. Thankfully, no one got on at the second or first floors. When at the ground floor, the doors opened. Peering into the lobby I caught the attention of a staff member and told him of my plight. I had to wait a further twelve minutes, or so, outside my room for the key to arrive. In all, my misadventure cost me fifteen valuable minutes, and my breakfast was cold: I was very annoyed. No time to fret about it though. After a few hurried mouthfuls of food, washed down by a cup of tea, I was on my way.

As usual, my first priority at the airport was to obtain a weather report, and as that looked reasonable, I lodged my flight plan. Next, it was immigration and customs procedures and before I knew it, I was striding across the tarmac towards *Margery* to load her up. I threw my new tube-in-pillow-case cushion into the cockpit and then managed the tricky, almost Houdini-like, feat of stuffing all of my luggage into the impossibly small space behind the cockpit called the baggage compartment. Besides my luggage, it also held spare oil, water, tie-down ropes, chocks and two cardboard boxes of spare parts.

As I turned around, one of the several ground-handlers, who had been in the airport terminal, came running across to me and said that immigration and customs now required an additional fee of US$50 and could I give it to him now to pay them. I knew full well that there was no such additional fee, and besides, guilt was written all over his face. So I said to him, "I have paid all that was required, but if you bring me an account showing this amount, I will pay it." He slowly turned and walked away and did not return before I took off. I pondered how many pilots in the past he had conned.

After refuelling, I radioed the tower for permission to start my engine and was dumbfounded to receive a reply that my flight plan had not been approved. I was sure it had been approved when I lodged it, but now they must be having second thoughts. Another two hours elapsed before I was able to restart, which made me angry and anxious. With the engine running, I carefully pulled the chocks, stowed them in the baggage compartment and jumped into the cockpit.

What must have been an unfriendly, scowling face (mine) suddenly turned into a wry smile as I found myself sitting a good four to five inches higher than usual, with my head sticking high out of the cockpit. I should have taken the existing seat cushion out first before inserting the tube cushion! 'Never mind,' I thought to myself, 'you have been delayed long enough, without now stopping the engine just to rearrange the seating', and so I prepared to taxi atop my new lofty seat. I just hoped it wouldn't impede me on the long flight ahead.

My clearance for take-off on RWY 04 included an unusual instruction that I climb to my cruising altitude of 6,500 feet directly above the airport. With RWY 04 designated right-hand circuits only, my climb was a seemingly never-ending series of climbing orbits in that direction. Under a full load of fuel, poor *Margery* was struggling, and it took twenty-five minutes to reach 6,000 feet. At that point, I couldn't wait any longer and called to the tower that I was now at cruising altitude. I think the controller must have had enough of the laborious effort also, and I was allowed to proceed immediately to Iraklion on the island of Crete.

The seaside concrete jungle of flats and apartments, where I had been just hours before, now passed beneath me as I headed out over the Mediterranean for the first time. The dreaded sea haze was getting thicker by the minute, but before I became too preoccupied with that, I had to discipline myself to carry out the usual cockpit tasks. These included marking times on my flight plan and chart, starting my fuel log and generally settling my mind into the trip ahead. Looking back over my shoulder for a last reassuring glimpse of Africa, it was gone.

Two hours into the flight and still not half way, the horizon was becoming very difficult to discern. I reassured myself by frequently looking directly over the side to the blue-grey sea below. It was fascinating watching the rolling waves which appeared to move in slow motion. By watching one wave long enough, I would see it eventually break and a small cascade of white would appear before disappearing. To me, the waves were like thousands of miniature episodes comprising a massive ocean, or in this case, the Mediterranean Sea. I never tired of looking at them, but now, with only a limited horizon, I couldn't afford to look over the side for long at all. Doing so couldn't tell me if my wings were straight and level, which became readily apparent when I started to experience some disorientation. As, on a number of occasions throughout the trip, the one flight instrument which could have dispelled this feeling and taken away the resultant anxiety and fear, was an artificial horizon. But I kept reassuring myself by thinking, 'Ah well, the pioneer aviators didn't have one either!'

On this occasion, while flying partly on instruments, I had been looking over the left side and to me the wings were level, but when I looked over the right side, the wings seemed to be at an angle to the water. 'Which side is straight and level?' I asked myself as I went into another cold sweat. Meanwhile, I had been drifting to the right and was now several miles off track. As, over the Red Sea, I managed to pull myself together again and set about getting on top of the situation. Apart from getting back on track, this entailed scanning the instruments properly, making use of the weakest of horizons when visible and not looking over the side for any reference. With everything now under control again, I treated myself to a biscuit and a few sips of water.

For the first time on the trip, the air was beginning to feel slightly chilly, and it became progressively cooler the further north I flew. My track would take me to Sitia at the eastern end of Crete before turning west for Iraklion. I was now 40NM south of Sitia and radio exchanges between Radar Control (Approach) and commercial (ATP) aircraft were considerable.

I wrote in my diary:

> *Approaching Iraklion there was a lot of traffic and I was concerned that they should know where I was, to be fitted in. The Approach guy got a bit angry with me and said he would not be offering me separation (being VFR) and the best he could do would be to advise Iraklion of my ETA.*

I thought his attitude was decidedly unfriendly and unwarranted, for my only concern was to make a safe approach to Iraklion. The captain of one airliner had obviously overheard my exchanges with Radar Control and struck up a brief conversation with me, asking me about the Tiger Moth and the purpose of my trip – it helped to break the tension. I guess I had also been a little on edge: flying for four or five hours over a large sea without sighting land, or having human contact, is a lonely and rather nerve-wracking experience. My diary continued:

> *On descent on the northern side of the island I noticed this large cloud bank, 5 Octas at less than 1,000 feet. Gave me quite a shock, but as I was coming down from 6,500 feet, I knew there was no way I could descend through the cloud, so did a few turns and an orbit to come in under it. This was a long, power-off descent and when I was finally under the cloud (600 feet AGL), the alternator light started to flicker. Remembering Jeddah, I quickly turned off all electrics for the next ten minutes to conserve what*

*battery power was left. I was now about 15NM inbound.*
*When I switched everything back on again, the alternator*
*light stayed off – thank goodness.*

The air traffic controller also decided to have a chat with
me, and before I knew it, I was on the ground after dealing
with a strong crosswind. Crosswinds and turbulence at Iraklion
are notorious. The Jeppesen Aerodrome chart I was using even
carried a warning – "TURBULENCE IN THE APPROACH,
TAKE-OFF AND CLIMB-OUT AREAS – Exercise extreme
caution as seasonal strong south-south easterly winds of more
than 20KTS prevail over and in the vicinity of the airport..." One
thing that had worked well on this leg was my seat cushion; I had
been almost pain free.

*Margery* was tied down securely for the night, and after
immigration formalities, I caught a taxi to my hotel. Since
Pakistan, none of my accommodation had been pre-booked –
I'd simply asked the taxi driver for his recommendation. Tonight,
I finished up in a spartan, no frills, 1960s style hotel. There was no
television and the décor was tasteless – brown vinyl floor coverings
and a lime-green bed spread. To cap it off, an invigorating cold
shower. But, I could not be happier, for I was now another step
closer to my goal. I walked into town and had a café meal, at the
same time watching Mexico versus Brazil in a World Cup soccer
match on a large television screen. The locals were glued to the
screen and there was very little talking. Iraklion had a relaxed,
comfortable feel about it and I enjoyed my two-hour sojourn into
the city.

Back at my hotel, I rang home and talked to Ali – she
was excited I was now in Europe and I was too. I also spoke to
John Roberts who suggested that my alternator problem today
might have been due to the long power-off descent, as well as
the alternator possibly only putting out around 13 volts. As had
been the case in Luxor, I rationalised (probably wrongly) that the

problem was not serious enough to hold me back, and so made the decision to push on to Corfu tomorrow. The closing comment in my diary:

> *Feel so close and yet still so far from England. Can't wait to get there now. Just hope and pray that Margery holds up for the last 6 legs – particularly the alternator/ battery.*

A fitful night's sleep frustrated my intention of being rested for the long day ahead, and the day didn't get any better. It was 14 June, day 50 of my journey. Since it was Sunday, the kitchen-hand was reluctant to give me an early breakfast, but finally relented when I told him the manager had promised it the night before. At the airport, I spent three hours going from one place to another, meteorological office, briefing office and immigration. No one was in a hurry, not even a hint of urgency, and there was an air of indifference to my journey and what I was trying to achieve. The one exception was the air traffic controller. Because I had to fly a different route from what I had originally planned, he was helpful in revising my flight plan. But, apart from him, as I wrote in my diary:

> *For some reason a lot of the Greek people were annoying the hell out of me today – I think it's their attitude to a small-time operator like me – they really don't want to know you.*

This feeling was further confirmed when, just prior to start up, a customs woman drove up and insisted I pay an almost 100 percent fuel tax because I was classified a private operator. She was a short, buxom, middle-aged woman with expressionless eyes, thin lips and a set square jaw. She was rather intimidating and reminded me of a teacher I had feared as a nine-year-old in

Author

*Late afternoon, Alexandria beach*

Author

*Paxois Island, Greece*

Author

*Base approach - Capodichino Airport, Naples*

Author

*Castel Dell'Ovo, Naples*

Author

*Gaeta, Italy - holiday resort & US Navy Base*

Author

*On finals - Cannes Mandelieu Airport*

Author

*Mt St Victoire, Aix-en-Provence, France*

Author

*Golfech Nuclear Power Station, France*

Author

*Abbeville - Sheep on airstrip*

Author

*Pierre Darras - President Somme Aero Club, Abbeville*

Author

*White Cliffs of Dover*

Unknown

*The journey ends. Marshalls Airport - Cambridge*

Courtesy Marshall Aerospace

*With welcoming English formation pilots L to R - Terry Holloway, Henry Labouchere, Mark Miller, Mike Vaisey, Author, Paul Chapman, Paul Szluha and Peter Jackson*

Courtesy Marshall Aerospace

*Exchanging crest and scroll with Mr Michael Marshall, CBE, DL, Chairman of Marshall of Cambridge (Holdings) Limited, and Vice Lord-Lieutenant of Cambridgeshire*

Courtesy Cambridge Evening News

*Hon. Clive Griffiths AO, JP, Agent General of the Government of Western Australia presenting letter from the Governor of Western Australia*

Courtesy Jock Hay

*Finally with Carol*

primary school! In response to my protests about this excessive charge, she replied through an interpreter, the fuel tanker driver, "You pay up or you don't move." I reckoned she could have torn a man in two if she'd wanted to.

And so, with my romantic feeling about Iraklion further diminishing, I decided not to stay a minute longer but to pay up and push on to my next destination – Kerkira on the island of Corfu. I was now left totally on my own to start *Margery*, carefully pull the chocks away and head out over the Mediterranean once more. But in my haste to get away, I didn't arrange my map, flight plan and various other bits and pieces as well as usual, and I spent most of the time on climb to my cruising altitude (6,500 feet) reorganising these items, which wasn't an ideal start.

Approximately 90 percent of today's 377NM leg would be over water as I had been re-routed away from mainland Greece. Winds at Kalamata, about the halfway mark, were forecast to be 15 knots from the north-west, which was of some concern, but at least I should be well above the forecast scattered cloud at 2,500 feet. Of greater concern, was the forecast for Kerkira with 15 knot westerly winds, rain showers in the area, scattered cumulonimbus cloud at 1,800 feet and broken cloud at 3,500 feet. True to the forecast, my ground speed for the first hour was only 55 knots, but it improved to 70 knots. My first position report over the small island of Kithira went unanswered, and there were no other aircraft in the area to relay my call. I continued on to the next reporting point of Cape Tenaro, which is near the town of Kainouryia Khora, on the southern tip of one of the narrow arms of land that protrude into the Mediterranean from the Peloponnese Peninsula.

*Margery* began to shake wildly, probably caused by a mountain wave formed by rapidly moving, turbulent air flowing around this southern tip of land. My main concern was the wings and I quickly changed course to the left, away from the land. After a mile or two, the turbulence subsided, but the wind remained strong and I began to feel cold, despite having an extra layer of clothing on. As I commenced the 30NM crossing of Messiniakos Gulf, tracking in a north-westerly direction, the water below was an inky, almost black colour, dotted with numerous white caps. It looked most uninviting, almost treacherous, and as with the desert, I shuddered at the thought of a forced landing in such conditions.

I likened my situation to that of a Second World War pilot flying alone on a sortie over the windswept Mediterranean, and I patted myself on the back for being something akin to them. But I quickly reminded myself that there was one crucial difference – they were flying in a hostile theatre of war with the very real threat of being attacked and possibly killed by the enemy at any moment. There was no comparison!

The cold was now starting to affect me, and to make life a little more comfortable I reduced my altitude to 2,500 feet. It felt marginally warmer at this height, but that was probably more a state of mind than anything else. Reaching the other side of the Gulf, I continued over a low mountain range which varied between 2,000 and 3,300 feet. The turbulence resumed and I had to hang on tight to *Margery* until we were once more over the water some twenty-five minutes later.

Zakinthos Island was my next destination, 45NM away, and in the distance I could see the cloud cover increasing. The alternator warning light had been coming on for the last half hour but, so far, I had managed to recycle it each time. I made an inbound call to Zakinthos Airport to say that I would be overflying, but as at Kithira, received no reply. For safety, I climbed back up to 5,000 feet before overflying the airport. I continued to make calls, but still no answer. Crossing the airport, I could clearly see an array of parked airliners and was glad to move away as quickly as I could.

Kefallinia Island lay 20NM ahead and my track would take me directly over a 5,341 foot peak at the southern end of the island. To clear it, I would need to be at a minimum altitude of 6,000 feet, but already I could see that would not be possible because of the dense cloud covering the island. To solve the problem, I diverted 5NM off track and travelled around the eastern coast of the island. But as I did so, there was a thunderstorm cell in my way and I decided I would try to fly between it and the island. As I flew past the cloud, which was now just 1 to 2NM away, *Margery* shook violently and I realised I had made a grave mistake and broken one of the most basic rules taught to all student pilots – to keep a safe distance from thunderstorms. Although they might seem innocuous, I can vouch for the fact that the power generated by these cells is enormous. Fortunately, we just received a short, sharp shaking, but it was enough to teach me a lesson for all time.

At this point, I was having difficulty in recycling the alternator. The red light was not going off and, even worse, was dimming. I was now 80NM from Corfu and so decided to turn off all electrics for the next hour and hope that when I turned everything back on again at 20NM, I would have sufficient battery power left to make the necessary inbound and circuit calls. Flying was now solely by dead reckoning – holding a steady heading of 330°, navigating by the islands and monitoring time and distance accurately. At 22NM I turned the electrics back on again, but to my alarm the red light was barely visible. I immediately contacted Kerkira tower, told them I was about to suffer a total radio failure and could they grant me a straight-in approach for runway 35, for I knew the wind was roughly from that direction.

The tower controller could not properly understand me and it was left to an airliner in the near vicinity to explain my problem. From my map, I had my position as just 2NM north-west of Paxoi Island. Straining my eyes, I could see a faint white strip of coast, far in the distance, some 20NM away, and comparing the shape of the island to that shown on my map, reckoned it must be Corfu. My eyes remained glued to this small white mark until I could confirm it was Corfu. The radio came back to life for a matter of seconds at both 10NM and 5NM, just enough for me to give my position and restate my intentions. Then on long finals, it came on again and thankfully stayed on. I couldn't believe it, and I don't think the controller could either!

Kerkira has just one runway, which extends out into a large lake-like body of water just in from the coast. Final approach was over the sea with the island on my left and a low mountain range running down the centre of it – highest peak 1,850 feet. As I came below the range, *Margery* began to buck on account of the disturbed air flowing around the mountains, but at this point was controllable. But on short finals, the mountain range gave way to flatter ground, and I suddenly became aware of a strong crosswind from my left. Crabbing into wind, I continued the approach until just past the threshold, and at only one or two feet from the ground, kicked in right rudder, applying left aileron at the same time to keep *Margery* travelling straight down the runway and to avoid being blown to the right. But the crosswind was much too strong to hold and blew *Margery* to the right anyway. Applying just enough power to keep the wheels from touching the tarmac, I again applied left aileron to bring us back over the centre line. There was no alternative runway and with my radio problem, I did not fancy a go-round. I just had to try and put her down.

By this stage, we had travelled a good 250 metres down the runway. Holding as much left aileron as I dared and keeping the nose straight, I descended lower to the runway this time, but, as before, was blown sharply to the right. I immediately knew it was too far when I saw an object appear from under the lower right wing and go barrelling down the runway ahead. 'Oh no,' I said to myself, 'that was a runway light!' I imagined a big rip in the fabric under the wing and possibly rib or spar damage. Bringing *Margery* back over the centre line, for what I hoped was the last time, I was finally able to plant the main wheels, and applying maximum left aileron and forward stick, just managed to stay on the runway and, even more importantly, to avoid being flipped over.

This had certainly been one of my more difficult legs, and the extreme conditions on landing hadn't made it any easier. As I departed the runway, it was as if a huge weight had been lifted from my shoulders. The feelings of stress and, on occasions, mild panic that had been with me for the past six hours or so, suddenly left me, and I found myself in a seemingly peaceful, safe environment. But though back on terra firma, I felt physically and mentally drained.

Bringing *Margery* to a stop in a parking area at the far end of the runway, I was anxious to climb out and inspect the damage caused by the runway light. To my great relief there was not even a mark. I could only assume that it was the right-hand main tyre that had clipped the light.

I went to the control tower to give a full account of the occurrences of this flight, including the radio failure and the fact that they hadn't received one position report en route. I was informed that the aviation authorities were so concerned that a C-130 Hercules had been sent from Athens to look for me, and only turned around again just 30NM from Corfu, at about the same time my first intermittent radio transmission was received by Kerkira tower. After overcoming my embarrassment on hearing this news, I expressed sincere gratitude for the concern shown for my well-being and the efforts they had gone to. Now that he'd seen *Margery*, and been made aware of the difficulties I'd experienced, the controller showed nothing but understanding and, I believe, a hint of sympathy. And there the matter was allowed to rest.

An extract from my diary entry reads:

*The Greek Islands are quite something and I'm staying*

*in a fine hotel tonight set on the side of a hill with great
views to the west and over the runway! Had a good meal
and looking forward to a day off, but will be working quite
hard at the same time to solve this electrical nightmare.
Feel that today's occurrences have put quite a dampener
on things – but I'm keen to bounce back.*

I slept poorly that night and was up several times with a
stomach complaint, which must have been caused by something
I'd eaten. Breakfast was out of the question and I stayed in bed
until 8.30am, feeling wretched rather than rested.

At the airport I met Christo, an engineer who had been
recommended as the only person at the airport who could,
perhaps, fix *Margery*'s electrical problem. (There was no aircraft
repair facility at the airport.) He was a short, stocky fellow with
neat grey hair, aged about sixty. His manner, at first, seemed a
little brusque, but he soon warmed to the idea of fixing a fault that
no one else had been able to fix so far. And I think he relished the
chance to work on such an old aeroplane as a Tiger Moth. With
his limited English, he told me he had worked on piston-engined
fighter aircraft in the 1960s.

After I'd explained to him, in some detail, the symptoms
of the problem, and that the general consensus had been that it
was the alternator, he quietly said, "I don't think so – everybody
always looks at the most complicated component first, but in my
experience, the answer is often a very simple one, such as a loose
wire." We decided it would be best to obtain the services of an
auto-electrician from town to assist Christo, but he wouldn't be
available until later in the day. Still feeling unwell, I went back to
the hotel and had a couple of hours sleep. I returned to the airport
around 2.00pm, and Christo and the auto-electrician were ready
to start work. In no time, they had located several loose wires
behind the control panel and tightened them – Christo was right!
The battery was recharged, and then it was time for an engine run.

I felt so weak I could barely swing the prop. However, everything seemed to be working fine and the red warning light was going out.

A weather report from the tower controller indicated poor weather over the Apennines for the next day, so I resigned myself to another day in Corfu. I was back at the hotel at 9.30pm and found a brief, heart-warming message from Carol, in England, under my door: "All the best for your journey – from your wife." I rang family at home, a great way to end the day, and my final diary note for the day read:

> Tomorrow I'm going to try and fix a couple of oil leaks on the engine and prepare thoroughly for the next leg to Naples, i.e. go over my flight plan and charts, get out my cold-weather gear and generally just make sure I'm right for the final 5 days flying.

After breakfast the following morning, I negotiated a sight-seeing tour of the island with George, a local taxi driver. Without telling me, his first port of call was a popular topless swimming beach. The area was busy with traffic, so we moved on without stopping. Just as well, for I am sure I would have felt more uncomfortable than the swimmers. My diary notes:

> Within the space of 2 hours, I saw some absolutely stunning views, Roman ruins, etc. There really is a lot to the island and you would need a week to take it in properly. Everything they say about Corfu in the tourist advertisements is true. The Old city (as opposed to the New) with 600-year-old buildings has a lot of atmosphere and I wish I could have stayed to try at least one of the hundreds of cafés and restaurants. But I had to be back at the airport by 3.00pm.

I started *Margery's* engine at 3.30pm, and a check by

Christo showed that the alternator was putting out in excess of 12 volts with the radios on. Following a few minor adjustments, I took off on a test flight just after 5.00pm. It was a one-hour jaunt that took me to Paxoi Island and back. The air was silky smooth, skies clear blue and the scenery around the deep green hinterland of the island just beautiful – expensive resort style buildings in the bays, and pristine white beaches gave way to turquoise shades near the shore and then the deep blue of the ocean. It was the most stress-free flight I had experienced since leaving home, both relaxing and exhilarating.

Upon landing, I confirmed with Christo that everything looked fine – the only electrical instrument I couldn't test was the transponder, as Corfu was yet to have radar, although it would have soon. The tower controller gave me some good advice on flying to Naples, and we arranged to have another chat in the morning. A weather report faxed from Perth by Sunny earlier in the day had shown a significant build-up of cloud on the west coast of Italy, and this was supported by a later fax from John Roberts – today certainly hadn't been the right time to go.

By now I was fully recovered and ready to tackle the final phase of the trip. Arriving at the airport the following morning, I first visited the meteorological office. An hour later they came up with their report, which showed storm activity near Gio Del Colle and, hence, instability was predicted over the Apennines. Their forecast for the following day was for much-improved weather, so I decided to stay. Feeling disappointed and frustrated, I checked back into the same hotel once more. Instead of getting on with tackling the Apennines, I would have to live with my apprehension of this crossing for one more night. Adding to this apprehension was the dread of the electrics failing again.

I spent the rest of the day sightseeing. George picked me up again and showed me some of the breathtaking coastline. It was a crystal-clear day and the temperature was 25°C (78°F).

The highlight was stopping for a coffee at the Golden Fox Café which forms part of the compact Paleokastritsa Hotel complex in the northern part of Corfu, on the west coast. It is situated on top of a hillside ridge, the slopes covered in olive and cyprus trees and smaller native plants, and overlooking the popular seaside resort area bearing the same name, Paleokastritsa. Its six bays, with white beaches and turquoise waters, were a contrast to the surrounding rugged coastline with its rocky outcrops and sheer cliff-faces. The predominant colour of the island landscape was deep green with a bluish tinge – probably the effect of the olive trees.

Paleokastritsa takes its name from a monastery originally built in 1228 on top of a rocky hill jutting out into the sea, and is joined to the coast by a narrow beach-head: it is almost an island. The existing monastery buildings are about one hundred years old and from my vantage point, high on the café verandah, I looked directly out over the hill, monastery building, adjoining resort area, and the continuing rugged coastline and deep blue Ionian Sea beyond. It was a spectacular sight.

Returning to my hotel, late in the afternoon, I had a radio interview with the ABC in Perth. As this was my final night in Corfu, I treated myself to dinner at the Faliraki, a modest café-style restaurant right on the waterfront looking across to mainland Greece. It was a picturesque and quiet location, and I enjoyed my hour or so there, watching boats and ships go up and down the waterway.

# Chapter 12

## CORFU TO ABBEVILLE

**Days 54-59** - 18 June 1998 to 23 June 1998

I got up at 5.00am the next morning and ate a cold, toasted ham-and-cheese sandwich that I'd ordered the night before and put in the fridge. At the airport, I obtained a weather report which at last looked reasonable. Without any further delay, I lodged my pre-prepared flight plan and departed just after 8.00am

With a track to Brindisi of 300°, I commenced the climb to my flight-planned cruising altitude of 6,500 feet. But the headwind was horrendous, and at one stage in the climb, *Margery*'s ground speed went as low as 37 knots. 'Going backwards,' I thought to myself. I knew from this it was going to be a very long haul – and it was. The maximum ground speed I achieved between Corfu and Brindisi was 50-55 knots.

Well before Brindisi, Radar Control advised me that if I wanted to overfly Gio Del Colle (a military base), as per my flight plan, then I would have to climb to 9,500 feet, or else detour via Bari and Sorrento. The latter option was unappealing, as it was indirect and would have added considerable time to the leg. I advised them of my decision to continue via Gio Del Colle, and was instructed to commence my climb to 9,500 feet "*now!*" – even though I still had some 20NM to run to Brindisi and then a further 45NM to Gio. I had the feeling they were testing me to see if *Margery* really could climb that high, or else they realised she was so slow, and were giving her ample time to crawl to the required altitude.

My diary recorded:

> *I was already at 6,500 feet and wearing thermal top, T-shirt, flying suit, jumper, jacket and woollen gloves, and feeling pretty cold, but at around 9,000 feet it was freezing. At 9,300 feet I detected carbie icing – the engine started missing – so I dropped about 100 feet, pulled back on the revs slightly and leaned the mixture. I couldn't go below 9,000 feet as I was already supposed to be at 9,500 feet, and was asked for confirmation of this several times. The engine missed at least a dozen times over this period, but thankfully didn't stop. I kept a good lookout for suitable forced-landing places, of which there were quite a few, as I was over a rural area.*

The cold was so intense I could feel it in my bones, and my face went numb. There was no running away from it, and I knew I was going to be in this situation for some time yet. The best I could do to combat the feeling was to tense my body, breathe slowly and evenly, and try not to think about it. The cold may have had an effect on my mental state, for while *Margery* was experiencing carbie icing, I couldn't have been calmer, and was almost blasé about the prospect of a forced landing. As I passed over the top of Gio Airport, I immediately requested a descent to 6,500 feet to try and gain relief from the cold, but permission was declined, and I had to maintain my present altitude of 9,300 feet for another 15NM.

When I was finally allowed to descend, the Apennines were starting to loom up, and cloud cover was increasing. I still had 75NM to run to my next reporting point of Pontecagnano on the west coast, all of which was over mountainous terrain. The cloud base was around 5,000 feet, and I tried to descend below it. However, with some of the terrain ahead rising to 5,700 feet, it was not long before the cloud was meeting the ground. I managed to pick a path between the large cloud masses for a while, until it began to close in around me. A quick 180° turn was the one and only answer – to try and find some sunshine. The cloud build-up increased by the minute – beautiful grey-white cauliflower masses, deadly dangerous to be trapped within.

There was one avenue left if I was to continue on westwards, and that was to climb above it. Spiralling slowly upwards between the cloud masses was a tricky exercise, as they were several thousand feet in depth and moving. Although concerned, I felt totally in control at this point, and just concentrated on flying *Margery*. I levelled out at 8,000 feet, just on top of the cloud. Once again, the cold started to bite, but it was just a matter of grinning and bearing it – at least it was 2°C warmer than when I was at 9,000 feet.

My only concern now, was that the cloud cover would thin sufficiently for my descent into Naples. Approaching Pontecagnano on the west coast, I was able to descend to 6,500 feet. I then turned right onto a track of 298° for the final 30NM to Naples. The coastal town of Salerno, on the gulf by the same name, lay directly ahead, and to its immediate left, a rugged mountain ridge peninsula with a high point of 4,739 feet, protruded into the Tyrrhenian Sea – it was an impressive sight. On part of the peninsula, I could just make out the Amalfi Coast, a popular tourist destination, further still and straight ahead, the faint outline of Mt Vesuvius standing at 4,203 feet. I was soon flying along the lower northern slopes of this mountain, and the view was stunning. I had lost contact with Rome Approach (flight controllers for this area) for ten minutes or so, and an Air Alitalia pilot, who had heard my repeated calls, finally came to the rescue and relayed a message for me.

I was now on descent to 1,500 feet, and Naples airport and runway were clearly visible. I was instructed to join base for runway 24, and as I did so, a large commercial jet commenced its take-off roll. The air had not properly settled by the time I reached short finals, and I blamed this for an awkward landing. But it was a great relief to be on the ground again after another long and testing flight. It took several hours to thaw out sufficiently to feel normal again – I had never felt so cold in my life over such a protracted period of time.

I finished tidying *Margery* up, and was preparing to tie her down for the night, when I was summoned to the Control Tower. I was bluntly told, that as I hadn't made prior parking arrangements, I would have to move on to another airport immediately. Under no circumstances could *Margery* stay where she was presently parked, even though I had been directed there after landing. According to the controller, parking in the open was at an absolute premium, and there wasn't enough room even for a Tiger Moth. I didn't believe him for one minute.

Feeling physically and mentally drained, I couldn't understand how anyone could be as cold and heartless as this person. Only just managing to keep my temper under control, I firmly told him that I wasn't going anywhere, *Margery* was staying put and I would leave in the morning. Following a short discussion with a colleague, he came back to me and said that the only way I could stay, would be if the Napoli Aero Club allowed me to park in their hangar for the night.

I had to wait an hour-and-a-half for the director to arrive and say yes or no. It seemed to be a poor set-up with ten or eleven aircraft, two mechanics and two office employees. Everyone worked without lights, in both the hangar and office, and there was a distinct lack of vibrancy about the place. All of the staff were pleasant to talk to though, notwithstanding the language difficulty. Eventually the director arrived – a short, slight man with swept-back, thinning grey hair, dressed in a smart mid-grey suit with collar and tie. He wasn't remotely interested in my mission when I explained it to him, and didn't smile once.

By this time, I'd had enough, and pointedly told him that I had been well received in almost every country I had passed through, except here. Finally, reluctantly he said, "You can lock *Margery* in the hangar overnight, but must leave in the morning – there will be no excuses." But that just fired me up even more, and I replied, "If the weather is bad and it is unsafe, I will not go." Where I would park would be another matter. I managed a "thank you", for I was at least relieved that *Margery* would be safe for the night.

At the air terminal, I mistakenly walked through the wrong gate, and it took me a full hour to be allowed air-side again. At this point, I was almost tearing my hair out, or what was left of it. My frustrations continued in the briefing office where they were insisting upon a complicated departure sequence. It meant I would have some homework to do that night, although a private pilot (who happened to be in the briefing office also lodging a flight plan), offered me some helpful advice.

My diary summed up the rest of the day:

> *Taxi driver took me on a long, unnecessary drive claiming he couldn't understand English and, all in all, I have just had so many run-ins with people today. Adding to the drama was the sight of a poor soul receiving CPR (cardio pulmonary resuscitation) on the footpath, as we passed through the city centre. I feel pretty tired and stressed out tonight, and have still not finalised what I need to do to get to Cannes. I think it's probably better if I go to bed now and get up early tomorrow for a fresh start. Had a nice meal on the waterfront next to Castel dell'Ovo, overlooking Mt Vesuvius.*

My alarm was set for 5.15am, and I awoke feeling energetic after a reasonable night's sleep. I was not looking forward to all I had to do to get out of Naples, but then decided there was only one way – tackle it head on and get stuck into it. And so I did, carrying out all the necessary alterations to my map, flight plan and GPS.

I met a couple of really friendly people at the Aero Club and had a brief, pleasant conversation with them. Flying solo on such a long journey is, by its very nature, a lonely experience, and having these occasional encounters with total strangers usually put me in a good frame of mind. With *Margery* refuelled, packed and ready to go, I requested permission to start over the radio, but was politely informed that I must first pay my airport charges before permission would be granted. This was no one's fault but my own, and I resigned myself to the one-kilometre walk and forty-minute delay to rectify the situation.

Today's flight of 364NM would be almost entirely over water, the Tyrrhenian and Ligurian Seas, and for this reason, I would carry almost maximum fuel, giving me a total endurance of close to 9.5 hours. A further reason for carrying so much fuel, was that I had been warned at the Briefing Office by the knowledgeable private pilot, that once I reached Latina on the west coast and made the obligatory request to Rome radar to cross the Tyrrhenian Sea to Bastia, permission might be denied, given the small size and antiquity of my aircraft, irrespective of my approved flight plan. The result could be that I would be made to travel a considerable distance up the western coast of Italy to minimise the water crossing to Cannes.

Commencing the take-off roll on runway 24, *Margery* felt very heavy, and we crawled into the air. I was concerned about the rising ground directly ahead, a hillside covered in residential homes and apartments. The attractive Mediterranean style of these dwellings, with walls of varying shades of white and cream and contrasting orange terracotta roof tiles, presented a beautiful picture. Maintaining 58 knots and avoiding the temptation to lift the nose higher, I worked hard to gain every foot of altitude I could. The roof tops were now only 300 to 500 feet below, and I could barely wait to commence the required right-hand turn to intercept the 325° outbound track. Not having an ADF or VOR, this was hardly a technical manoeuvre, and relied more upon gut instinct and experience than anything else. The maximum permissible altitude of 1,000 feet for the next hour-and-a-half or so, meant low-level flying over wonderful scenery – countryside with lush green pastures, rolling hills and quaint villages dotted here and there.

Tracking for Gaeta on the coast, I entered a valley on the wrong side of a low line of hills and wasted a good twenty minutes extricating myself and getting back on track. As I approached Gaeta, its unique geographical features, which make it one of the most popular holiday destinations along the Tyrrhenian coast, became clearly visible. A long isthmus of land extends out into the sea and southwards, creating a natural port. The grey, rocky face of Mt Orlando stood out in the centre of the isthmus, its emerald green eastern slope falling gradually to the sheltered waters of the Gulf. Lining the shores were numerous houses and holiday accommodation, their earthy cream and orange colours highlighted by the midday sun. Completing the picture, was the almost still, deep-blue sea and a near cloudless sky of lighter blue. Contrasting with this beauty, was the stark outline of a grey coloured warship tied up at its mooring. It was the USS *LaSalle*, flagship of the US Sixth Fleet, which has resided in Gaeta since 1994. Its primary role is to act as a command ship for the Sixth Fleet's commander and his staff, the majority of whom are accommodated in Gaeta with their families.

I continued on to Terracina. The next reporting point should have been Latina, a military base, but Latina Approach insisted that I divert out over the sea to another reporting point, presumably

IFR (instrument flight rules), of which I had no details. I was also now at the point where I should track directly for Corsica across the Tyrrhenian Sea, but first needed a clearance to do so.

I was worried that clearance would be denied, and decided to try to bluff my way through. Unable to determine the position of my last compulsory reporting point, I called Latina Approach and said, "Latina Aproach, this is Tiger Moth VH-NOV, from my present position, request direct track for Bastia Poretta."

"VH-NOV, stand by," came back the reply, but after two or three minutes had elapsed they hadn't contacted me.

As far as I was concerned, I was on my way and, now at my prescribed cruising height of 1,500 feet, I called them again saying, "Latina Approach, this is VH-NOV, from present position tracking direct for Bastia Poretta, maintaining 1,500 feet, estimate Bastia Poretta ..."

At this point they must have reasoned that as I was apparently already on my way, it was probably just as easy to let me continue, for they came back confirming my onwards track, and stating that I should call Bastia Approach 70NM D.M.E., reporting 'OPS Normal'. It was also at this point I was permitted to climb to a reasonable altitude. Heading out over the sea at just 1,500 feet had made me a little nervous, and for the very first time, I experienced phantom engine problems. I had heard of pilots having similar experiences when over water, but never thought that I would be a victim of it. What I was sensing were abnormal engine vibrations, possibly from the propeller, which were causing the whole aeroplane to shake – at least that is what my mind was telling me. But I was finding it hard to determine the degree of difference between the normal vibrations one feels when flying a Tiger Moth, and what I was feeling here and now. In truth, the difference was probably little or nothing, and I concluded that perhaps I was not flying *Margery* as accurately and smoothly as I could. And so I reduced the throttle slightly, leaned the mixture a touch, held a steady course and altitude, and the vibrations suddenly decreased and everything seemed normal!

I reported overhead Bastia, and then flew on over the northern tip of Corsica, crossing a rugged, mountainous landscape and passing just south of the Gulf of Saint-Florent. I was now flying over the Ligurian Sea and the cloud was increasing, but did not pose a problem being 3 Octas (three-eighths cloud cover) of stratocumulus at about 3,000 feet and visibility 8 to 10 kilometres. My ground speed was 70-75 knots, and I could feel my body starting to relax, knowing that the worst of this leg was over and in about an hour-and-a-half I would be in Cannes.

The approach to Mandelieu was straightforward, as the airport was situated close to the coast and clearly visible. With a light southerly breeze blowing, I touched down on runway 17. Surrounded by hills and green farmlands, it was one of the prettiest little aerodromes I have ever seen. The flight had taken just over five-and-a-half hours, and as usual, I was feeling tired and stiff from the cramped confines of the cockpit.

These feelings soon subsided, though, when I approached an airport staff member for directions. I was impressed by her pleasant smile and the genuinely warm welcome she gave to a comparatively old and bedraggled Aussie traveller who was setting foot in France for the very first time. I couldn't help comparing this welcome to the one I'd received in Naples. And this was my experience of almost everyone I encountered in France – warm, friendly people who were keen to help.

After refuelling *Margery,* I went to the Operations Room to lodge my flight plan for Toulouse. The person I spoke to couldn't have been more helpful, and I spent the next half hour with him, going over every aspect of the route I would take, including radio frequencies and, in particular, the caution I needed to exercise when overflying the military airport of Salon, and near the approach path of Marseille/Marignane Airport.

As usual, I asked the taxi driver to take me to a reasonable hotel for the night. All I needed was a shower, a decent meal and a comfortable bed. And it ended up being just that, with a number of the guests being young families and backpackers. My final diary entry for the day read:

> *Feel very happy to be in France, and Cannes in particular*
> *– it is basically a similar standard of people and living to*
> *Perth – civilisation at last!*

I was up at 6.30am the following morning after a restless night's sleep, which I put down to the demanding flying of the previous day, especially the departure from Naples and the Italian mainland. At the airport, I drained off 20 litres of fuel, as I was concerned that with only a four to five hour flight and carrying 9 hours of fuel, *Margery* would be heavier than necessary on arrival at Toulouse. It had always been my experience that it was easier to effect a good landing in a Tiger Moth that was on the lighter side – the controls were more responsive, and the aircraft more manoeuvrable.

I departed runway 17 with a near cloudless sky above, and tracked out over the Golfe de la Napoule, making a right hand turn at 800 feet. It was a beautiful picture – the rich greenery of the mainland, the blue Mediterranean and a low, rugged mountain range on the west side of the Golfe that fell sharply to the sea. Climbing over this range, I headed for departure point "WC". Some fifty minutes later, a prominent, knife-ridged mountain rose out of the landscape. From my position, its scale and beauty were stunning; the symmetrical wave-like pattern in its grey, granite surface, interspersed with small patches of dark-green vegetation in the upper levels which increased in density on the lower slopes. It was Mount Sainte-Victoire, 3,317 feet in height and situated just east of the town of Aix-en-Provence. It was made famous by the nineteenth century artist Paul Cézanne, who was captivated by its beauty and painted it many times.

I eased *Margery* to the right to take a closer look and travel the full length of the southern slopes. Directly below me was the small town of Bramefan, and half-way up the rugged slopes, I could make out the Chapel Saint Ser, nestled in its own green patch. The surrounding countryside was a rich patchwork of dark greens and light browns, representing the mixture of farmlands and vineyards which predominate in the region. Passing the western extremity of Mount Sainte-Victoire, the Rigaud, or Bimont Dam, came into view. It was also impressive with its high and narrow dam wall holding back a full reservoir of bright blue water.

At 15NM from Salon, a recorded radio message stated that aircraft were not permitted to overfly the airfield, and to keep south. I immediately complied. When abeam Aix-en-Provence Airfield, 5NM to the south, I tried to make contact with Marseille Information on 127.72, as advised by the Briefing Office. This was important, for within the next ten minutes or so, I would be crossing the approach path to Marseille/Marignane Airport. After several attempts, Marseille Information finally responded, and I was advised to maintain my current heading and height of 5,500 feet.

I could hear incoming traffic over the radio, and when close to the approach path scanned the sky with an eagle eye. Then far to my right, I sighted a speck, and I was astonished to see it growing rapidly larger and seemingly heading straight for me. In no time, the outline of a large jet airliner was clearly discernible. It passed directly beneath me on descent into Marseille. My nerves were on high alert, and I squeezed the throttle forward half an inch to get out of this zone as quickly as possible. Before I could though, another speck appeared, this one eventually passing just behind and below. Although a safe separation and under radar supervision, I found flying in such close proximity to a large, converging aircraft to be an alarming, if not exciting, experience. The horror stretch was over, and I hoped the remaining three hours would not cause any problems.

As I overflew Montpellier, I could see a huge blanket of cloud covering the Golfe du Lion to my left, the boundary of which was a clearly defined line along the coast. Although it was only a few miles away, I remained in clear skies. Within 8NM of Carcassonne, as I was preparing for the final 50NM run into Toulouse, the Approach Controller called me saying there was a message from a Mike Gibbs who would like me to divert to Auch. He added that he was a friend of Mike Vaisey of Vintech. Mike Vaisey had mentioned to me, in a phone call about a week earlier, that Mike Gibbs would meet me in Toulouse. The controller told me the approximate position of Auch – 33NM east of Toulouse/ Blagnac Airport, my planned destination. I located the airfield on my map, and also on my GPS, and quickly worked out a straight-line diversion that would take me just south of Toulouse/Blagnac Airport. It added another thirty-five minutes to my flight time, but I didn't mind and had ample fuel.

Auch, with a population of around 26,000, is situated in the Gascony region of south-west France, just over ninety kilometres north of the Spanish border and Pyrenées Mountains. Its history dates back to Roman Gaul when it was one of the main towns, and it was the capital of Armagnac in the tenth century, and Gascony in the seventeenth century. Auch remains an important farming and commercial trade centre today.

The track to Auch was across beautiful, undulating, green farmlands. I made inbound calls at 20NM, 10NM and then 5NM, but received no response. Apart from some higher-level stratocumulus cloud, visibility was good, and there was about a 15 knot easterly wind blowing. With a north-south oriented runway, I knew my crosswind landing technique was going to be tested once more. But first I had to find the airfield. My attention was taken by two brilliant turquoise-coloured dams in close proximity to one another, the effect, I was later told, of algal bloom.

At 3NM I heard radio chatter, but still no one was responding to me. My diary entry picks up from this point:

> *Didn't see Auch until I was almost on top of it, and was alarmed to see a tug and glider just taking off. There was no response to my repeated calls to the tower on 123.0, so I overflew and landed on runway 19. Very strong crosswind – almost to the max. Really had to hold Margery into it.*

Such was the effort of controlling this landing, that my right door popped open from the force of my shoulder – I'd never heard of a shoulder being part of a crosswind landing technique, but I'd employed excessive body language as part of mine!

Mike Gibbs came running out to greet me and looked very much at home wearing a rather worn, white panama hat. He was an Englishman who had lived in Auch for some years and spoke fluent French. Although there is a control tower, it is not constantly manned, and the airfield seemed to be an ideal location for the small group of aviation enthusiasts who operated from there with just a handful of aircraft. After helping me push *Margery* into a hangar, Mike bought me a beer in the bar, which was officially closed. It went down extremely well, and we swapped a few Tiger tales, Mike having been a Tiger owner at one time.

We drove for a quarter of an hour, through winding roads and the beautiful green farmlands I'd seen from the air, to Mike and his wife Chantelle's home. It was an 1830 house, which they had renovated in an idyllic country setting of three acres. Chantelle prepared a fine meal and we spent a pleasant couple of hours chatting. One chilling piece of news Mike broke to me, however, was the recent disappearance of Roger Fiennes when flying his Tiger Moth across the English Channel. This had a sobering effect on me. I was yet to cross the Channel, and it was a tragic reminder that flying is inherently dangerous, and that I must continue to be on my guard and to exercise caution.

Mike brought out some charts covering the remainder of my route through France, and offered helpful advice, especially when flying in the Paris region. When Mike Vaisey phoned to discuss some of the plans for my arrival in England, it dawned upon me how close I was getting. It became even more realistic when I then spoke to Carol, who was patiently waiting for me. I had also managed to telephone April earlier in the day, prior to leaving Cannes.

My diary entry for the following morning read:

> *Being Sunday 21 June and not flying today, got up after 8.00am and had breakfast at 8.30. This, I think, was my longest sleep-in for the whole trip. Worked on the flight plan for tomorrow and have decided to go on to Abbeville instead of Toussus (Paris). It increases my flight time from about 4 and a half hours to 6 hours, but according to Michael (Gibbs) it is a far more desirable destination.*

I carried out my planning seated at their dining table, next to two large timber doors which opened out onto a typical country garden with flourishing green shrubbery, neat manicured lawns, and black and brown hens blissfully strutting around looking for food. Completing this picture was the backdrop of beautiful French countryside. I felt totally relaxed and could not have been happier.

Mike Vaisey telephoned again to say that several Cambridge Flying Group members were hoping to fly to Abbeville in Tiger Moths with the object of meeting up with me. Their choice of town was a coincidence, as I had only made up my mind that day to fly to Abbeville. Unfortunately, the rendezvous did not eventuate – one of the Tigers had an altercation with a fence post at Headcorn aerodrome, and as they had wanted to fly as a team, decided to abort the trip across the Channel. My heart went out to them that their well intentioned plan did not come to fruition, but I was looking forward to an even bigger rendezvous in a few day's time. I managed to speak to Carol again as she was staying with the Vaiseys, and we were both excited that it would soon all be over. John Roberts also rang and was equally enthusiastic about my forthcoming arrival in England.

Chantelle prepared a sumptuous lunch of roast duck breast, a staple in this area, and we shared a bottle of red wine – a memorable meal with warm, friendly people. During the afternoon, I refuelled *Margery* and carefully checked her over for the next day's flight. There were thunderstorms in the vicinity of the airport, resulting in a couple of heavy downpours – I hoped it would clear up by tomorrow.

In the morning, I wrote in my diary:

> *After a restless night's sleep, I got up at 6.20a.m. I think it was the excitement that kept me awake. I can't believe that I'm nearly there – but I'm certainly not going to rest on my laurels, and will be concentrating right up until the wire.*

There were a number of officials and plain clothes police at the airport, apparently awaiting the arrival of a French Minister of Parliament from Paris. When he did finally arrive, I took the opportunity of asking the pilots about the weather conditions in Paris and en route. They said it was gradually improving, though suggested I wait at least another two hours before departing. Indeed, low dark clouds still surrounded the airport. Realising the importance to me of traversing the Paris area safely, they gave me a map of the area to supplement the one I was already carrying. In return, I gave them gold kangaroo pins – the last I handed out on the trip.

I was dressed up in my flying suit and ready to go, but the existing cloud cover and the ever-present urge to push on regardless, only served to make me anxious. I tried to sit down and relax, but this soon gave way to pacing up and down the airport terminal, burning up excess nervous energy. I knew that if I took off too soon, I could get caught in cloud, and the rational side of my brain won out. I finally took off at 11.50am in reasonable conditions. My planned cruising altitude of 4,500 feet was quickly amended to 2,500, since the cloud base was at 3,000 feet.

The countryside was beautiful, with rolling green hills and quaint villages dotted here and there. Twenty minutes after take-off, I unexpectedly came across two large bell-shaped towers located on the banks of the Gironde River. Two equally large plumes of white smoke were gently billowing from them. They seemed out of place in this otherwise serene setting. I was later to learn it was the Golfech Nuclear Power Plant operated by Electricité de France. Had I realised this earlier, I would not have flown as close as I did to take a photograph.

The French radar and tower controllers were very obliging and friendly, which helped ease the tension of flying over foreign territory. My track took me first to Sarlat and then on to Limoges, Châteauroux, Orleans, Toussus-le-Noble, Pontoise, Beauvais and finally Abbeville – a total of 400NM. Apart from being a long flight, there was a lot of buffeting on account of flying just under the cloud base at 2,500 feet, and there were a number of small cumulonimbus cells around.

Approaching the Paris region, I made the required inbound calls, and my eyes and ears were well and truly open for any traffic that might be around. To my surprise, it was very quiet, and I continued on without any problems. Before too long, the Paris skyline appeared to my right, perhaps just 7NM away, and I strained my eyes to see the Eiffel Tower. Along with the Great Pyramids in Egypt, it was a landmark I had most wanted to see from the air. And there it was, its shape unmistakable, standing proudly and in contrast to the modern shapes of other city buildings. I was so enthralled, I removed my goggles so I could say I'd seen it with my own eyes!

Crossing the River Seine, I continued on to Pontoise and Beauvais. The further north I flew, the colder it became, and I started to feel uncomfortable, not just from the cold, but also because of my bladder. All I could do was hold on. With about an hour still to run, it was going to involve a determined mental effort – perhaps I could think of apple pies, or roses, or something. Also, I hadn't eaten since about 6.45am and it was now late afternoon, but I had managed to sip water at regular intervals.

Abbeville came into view at last, and from the aerodrome diagram on my knee, and from the fact that it had an into-wind grass runway, it seemed a perfect choice. Since it was unmanned, it was up to me to execute the correct entry and to make the necessary "all stations" calls. Arriving over the top of the aerodrome, I was amazed to see a few hundred sheep grazing on one half of my preferred runway, so I altered course immediately to execute a landing on the main concrete runway (RWY 21). A hefty crosswind was blowing, but I still managed a reasonable landing.

This was my third landing point in France, and its beauty struck me immediately, as had been the case in Cannes (Mandelieu) and Auch. Sections of the renowned German Luftwaffe fighter unit, Jagdgeschwader Schlageter, or as it was more commonly known, JG26, were based here during World War II where they were equipped with Messerschmitt Bf109 (Me109) and later Focke-Wulf 190 (FW190) aircraft. Their pilots were respected by the British and American pilots who engaged them in combat, and they became known as "The Abbeville Boys". The concrete runway I had just landed on was the original. I taxied up to a row of old corrugated iron hangars adjoining the runway, and several people came out to meet me. They were members of the Somme Aero Club and offered me hangarage for the night without hesitation – such hospitality.

I booked into the motel on the airfield precinct overlooking the runways and surrounding green fields. The motel owner was a medium-sized, portly man of about forty with thinning, light-brown hair and a round, chubby face with rosy cheeks and a friendly smile. Although the language barrier made communication difficult, he was most helpful and made me feel welcome.

The concluding comment in my diary entry read:

> *Had a really nice steak for dinner – overlooking the field
> – watching the sheep being controlled by two sheep dogs
> to keep them off the main runway. A really lovely place
> which I would like to come back to one day. Some solid
> preparation now for my final day – can't wait.*

My alarm woke me at 6.00am, and as soon as I looked out of the window, I knew that my chances of departing today would be slim. Forecasts received from Sunny and John Roberts tended to support that. I was in limbo until getting final conclusive confirmation from the Cambridge Flying Group at 1.20pm. With cloud bases of 400, 600, 800 and 1,200 (BKN), it was now a definite no-go, as the minima or lowest permitted height for crossing the Channel is 1,200 feet. I felt frustrated that I could not get away, but felt more sorry for those who had already assembled at Cambridge to greet me, especially Carol.

Pierre Darras, the President of the Somme Aero Club, came over to have a chat and presented me with a couple of club decals which I was delighted to place on *Margery's* fuselage. After showing me around their facilities, he drove me to the Met. Office to check on the forecast for the next day. It was a lot better, but a cold front was expected later in the day, so I would need to aim to be on the ground at Cambridge no later than 1.00pm. With nothing left to do or prepare, I decided to walk into the town of Abbeville, about four kilometres. I walked at a leisurely pace, relaxing and taking in the beauty of the surrounding countryside. About a kilometre from the town, Pierre spotted me as he drove along the same road and gave me a lift the rest of the way.

Situated on the Somme River, Abbeville seems very old, and has an inviting feel to it, with street-side cafés and a large town square. It has a population of around 25,000 and its centrepiece is the late-Gothic Church of St Wolfram. A section of the church was badly damaged by a German Stuka dive bomber in World War II, and is currently undergoing restoration. I bought a pear and two bananas from a fruit store, sat down on a wooden bench, and thoroughly enjoyed them. I think my body craved them, as I had not eaten fresh fruit for about a fortnight. After spending an hour or so in the town – just sufficient to soak up some of the atmosphere – I headed back to the airport.

Before going to bed, I spoke to Carol again and assured her I was going to make it tomorrow, as the latest forecasts confirmed a weather window about mid-morning, which I fully intended to take. I was looking forward to a good sleep, as last night's had been restless – no doubt from excitement.

# Chapter 13

# ABBEVILLE TO CAMBRIDGE

**Day 60** - 24 June 1998

For the last time, I hoped, I awoke to my watch alarm at 6.00am, and immediately peered out of the window. The sky looked reasonable and I knew I would be departing today. However, I couldn't afford to waste any time, as weather reports received from John Roberts back home, and from the Cambridge Flying Group, showed a large low pressure system moving in from the west, and if I didn't make it across today, it might be another three days before it cleared. Over Abbeville, the cloud cover was scattered stratocumulus at 2,500-3,000 feet, quite safe for me to take off and head towards the Channel. Pierre and a few other people from the hangar were there to farewell me, and I took off into a light breeze on runway 21 at precisely 10.10am. Turning left, I circled back over the runway and returned a wave to the small group still standing in front of the hangar. I soon reached my cruising altitude of 2,500 feet, and tracked over a carpet of green farmlands for Le Touquet near the coast. Passing over Le Touquet right on time, I headed for Cape Gris Nez only 21NM away, and my departure point from France.

Tracking up the coast, I looked out to the left across the English Channel, and my heart picked up a beat or two – I would soon be across it! Cape Gris Nez was easily recognisable as a blunt point protruding out into the Channel. As I crossed the coast, I looked down and could see small waves gently lapping on the shore, and out a little, two or three sand bars showing through the clear blue water. My eyes were straining to see the White Cliffs of Dover, but because of the haze, all I could pick out were one or two ferries and several smaller vessels.

Then, only a few minutes later, a faint, long white line appeared. A lump came to my throat. I quickly suppressed it, telling myself there was still well over an hour to run, and that my concentration must be at its peak, right up until the last.

I made contact with Manston Radar, and was almost mesmerised by the White Cliffs of Dover as their image grew larger and larger the closer I got. I crossed the English coast and the White Cliffs at a point just west of Fan Bay. To my immediate left was Dover Harbour and breakwater, with the town behind. Further away, to the right, I could make out the smaller town of St Margaret's at Cliffe. The colour contrast of the rich green farmlands abutting the pure white cliffs, and then the blue waters of the Channel was beautiful. For me, the cliffs felt like the finishing line, and to cross them and be over English soil, was a momentous occasion.

But more was to come. The pressure was starting to ease, and I was in a controlled state of excitement. An aircraft in the near vicinity, hearing my radio exchanges with Manston, passed on his congratulations, and I appreciated the gesture. Visibility was good, but far to the north and west, there was a broad band of dark grey cloud, which had the appearance of a large blanket, that was about to roll in. It had a distinct edge, and I knew this must be the cold front that had been forecast. I felt secure in the knowledge that I would be safely down before it arrived.

Next it was Essex Approach, and passing to the west of London, I continued northwards before being handed over to Luton Approach. The controller gave me a cheerful welcome, and then liaised between myself and a formation of seven vintage de Havilland aircraft to facilitate the pre-planned rendezvous over Royston. I throttled back slightly and commenced a wide orbit of the town, which was clearly defined below me. And then it was into the second orbit, my eyes straining to catch a first glimpse of the lead aircraft, and my heart racing in quiet anticipation. Finally, Mike Vaisey's red and cream Tiger Moth G-APLU came into view, with Mike flying and Stuart McKay, secretary of the de Havilland Moth Club, his passenger.

As planned, I slotted in behind Mike at a safe distance, with the remainder of the formation falling in behind me and consisting of:

| No. 3 | DH82 | Tiger Moth | G-MOTH | Paul Szluha |
| No. 4 | DH87B | Hornet Moth | G-AHBL | Terry Holloway |
| No. 5 | DH87B | Hornet Moth | G-AELO | Mark Miller |
| No. 6 | DH82A | Tiger Moth | G-BPAJ | Peter Jackson |
| No. 7 | DH82A | Tiger Moth | G-APAL | Paul Chapman |
| No. 8 | DH82A | Tiger Moth | G-BEWN | Henry Labouchere |

Flying over Cambridge airfield, I glimpsed the classic architecture of the Control Building built in 1937, a signal for me to break left and descend for a crosswind entry to the grassed runway 24. A moderate breeze was blowing, and my primary concern now, was to make sure my last landing was a good one.

Turning base I spotted the threshold, not taking my eyes from it as I automatically brought my speed back to 65 knots and adjusted the trim. On finals, I maintained 60-62 knots as I wanted to fly *Margery* smoothly onto the grass rather than drop her in. Crossing the threshold, I eased the throttle back, and holding off with minute movements of the stick, *Margery*'s main wheels finally settled onto the grass. Then the familiar muffled, rumbling sound and accompanying vibration through the airframe as we travelled along, tail up, washing off sufficient speed before allowing the tail to settle. Leaving the runway, I said a quiet prayer of thanks, not just for a safe flight and landing, as I usually did, but for arriving safely in England! One by one the formation landed behind me.

The runway is a considerable distance from the parking area, and it seemed to take an eternity to reach the small crowd I could see in the distance. As I got closer, two marshals in orange vests took a wing tip each and guided me the last 50 metres or so to my parking position. Coming to a stop, on the grass in front of the Control Building, I carried out my magnetos check and shut the engine down.

In an instant, my throat went tight and I could feel my eyes welling up. Keeping my goggles on, I carried on with a few unnecessary cockpit tasks until the feeling subsided, for the last thing I wanted was an emotional display: this was a happy occasion. If my eyes did show it, then it was more than likely the wind had got under my goggles! My feelings at this point were a mixture of sheer exhilaration and great relief – *Margery* and I had made it!

My first priority was Carol, and looking across to my left, there she was, just a few metres away, walking towards me. She leaned into the cockpit and we embraced each other tightly. It was a wonderful moment. A man could not have wished for better support from a wife. She had shown great strength and fortitude throughout.

As I climbed from the cockpit, a number of people were gathered to meet me, including Mr Michael Marshall CBE, DL, Chairman of Marshall of Cambridge (Holdings) Limited, and Vice Lord-Lieutenant of Cambridgeshire; the Hon. Clive Griffiths AO, JP, the Agent General of the Government of Western Australia;

Terry Holloway, Group Support Executive of Marshalls; Peter Northover, General Manager of the Royal Flying Doctor Service of Australia (WA Division) and his mother. (Peter had just recently completed his term of duty as Aide-de-Camp to the Governor of Western Australia and had been in that position when I departed Langley Park); Bill Ison, CFI of the Cambridge Flying Group; Jock Hay, friend and Tiger Moth instructor at the Cambridge Flying Group; my brother Roger and his wife Dianne; and my nephew James Brearley and his wife to be, Tracy.

Clive Griffiths, on behalf of the Government of Western Australia, had kindly turned on a reception for me on the grass near where I had stopped – hors-d'oeuvres and champagne – a really thoughtful gesture. As I had arrived a day late, the Mayor of Cambridge was, unfortunately, committed elsewhere and unable to accept the scroll I had carried from the Town of Cambridge in Perth, as originally planned, but I was honoured to have this duty performed by Michael Marshall on behalf of the Mayor. In exchange for the scroll, he gave me a crest of the City of Cambridge, to be presented to the Town of Cambridge when I returned home. (I later received a crest for myself.) He also presented me with a book entitled *The Marshall Story – A Century of Wheels & Wings,* written by his father, Sir Arthur Marshall. It was an appropriate gift, as amongst other things, it detailed the history of the development of the airfield on which we were now standing. The Marshall family were, and still are, instrumental in the airfield's successful operation.

Clive Griffiths then presented me with a letter of congratulations from the Governor of Western Australia, His Excellency Major General Michael Jeffrey, AC MC. I was touched to receive such recognition, and it made me feel proud to be an Australian.

A number of television and radio reporters were present, and in between having photos taken with the formation pilots and crews, family and friends, I spent the next hour or so giving interviews. There was a buzz of excitement in the air and everyone appeared to enter into the spirit of the occasion. I was over the moon, and couldn't have been happier.

It was now time to put *Margery* away for a thoroughly deserved rest and push her the final 150 metres or so to the Cambridge Flying Group hangar, a blister hangar built in the 1930s. My faithful ship had served me well, and apart from the rain damage received in Sumatra, had managed to get through unscathed. I, too, was feeling fit and strong, even though I had shed 8kg in weight.

A surprise was in stall for Carol and me, as Mike Vaisey had booked us into the De Vere University Arms Hotel, a beautiful old hotel with our room overlooking a park, and flowers and champagne waiting for us in the room – a wonderful gesture for which we were most grateful.

I had been looking forward to a real English cup of tea for some time, and this we shared with brother Roger, his wife Dianne and Jock Hay in the hotel lounge before heading off for one last television interview.

For the conclusion of this momentous day – day 60 of the journey, I wrote in my diary:

> *Came back (from interview) and had a really nice meal in an elevated patio of a nearby café owned by Bill Wyman, a member of the Rolling Stones. It was a bit nippy, so they turned on an outside gas heater for us which was really effective. Just as we finished our meal, it started to rain – good timing. The manager also gave us complimentary glasses of champagne when Carol told him about the trip. Got back to hotel at around 11.00pm, but too excited to sleep. Talked a lot, and finally got to bed at 2.00am.*

# CONCLUSION

And so the journey ended. It is a chapter in my life that will live with me forever. There is hardly a day that goes by that I do not think of some aspect of my trip. It might only be a fleeting moment, but the thousand and one memories are indelibly etched in my brain and are never far from my conscious thoughts.

The high points far outweighed the low, and I shall never forget the vastness and rich colours of the Pilbara and Kimberley regions of Western Australia; the beauty of the Indonesian and Greek Islands with their green hinterlands, white beaches, surrounded by turquoise to deep blue seas; the harshness and stark beauty of the seemingly endless yellow-brown sands of the Saudi Arabian and Egyptian deserts; the Great Pyramids near Cairo; the Apennine Mountains and Mount Vesuvius in Italy; the patchwork of neat and ordered farmlands in Italy and France; the Eiffel Tower and Mount Sainte-Victoire in France; sighting the White Cliffs of Dover for the first time; and the tranquillity of flying on top of a carpet of white cloud with a brilliant blue sky above.

But above all, I shall never forget the dozens of people I met from many different ethnic backgrounds and beliefs, who seemed to possess, almost without exception, the inherent desire to want to help a fellow human being from the opposite side of the world who was on a strange journey.

*Margery* and I took exactly 60 days and 172.3 flying hours to travel through sixteen countries and cover a total distance of 10,951NM, or 20,281 kilometres. This equates to an average ground speed of 63.56 knots (117.71km) per hour, and there were 35 stops in all. By comparison, a Boeing 747 will typically fly from Perth to London at an average ground speed of 500 knots (926km) per hour, and making just two stops – Singapore and London. The total distance covered by the 747 is also considerably less on account of its more direct route.

I had started with a dream, set a goal and then achieved it. From the beginning, I was totally committed to achieving this goal, and the fear of failure was perhaps my main driving force. The physical and mental tests were many, more than I could ever have imagined, and they extended me fully. A university lecturer had once said to our group, "Whatever you believe is your maximum ability or potential, there is usually in everyone, another ten percent you can draw upon." I believe I dipped into that ten percent soon after leaving Australia! It was also not long after leaving Australia that I realised, if I was going to make it, then something bigger and better than me was going to get me through. The situations I found myself in over Sumatra, and then the Singapore Straits, were more than a wake-up call – they were plain frightening, and I know that my prayers were answered both times.

In helping me achieve my goal, standing firmly behind me, was a wonderful family and a close group of friends to whom I shall be eternally grateful.

My dream, which Carol had likened to a Walter Mitty fantasy, had been fulfilled, and was a testament to the words written from her heart and painted on my cockpit door: "Walter, fly high and safe, and live your dream today."

# AFTERWORD

The Royal Flying Doctor Service (RFDS) connection with my trip was important to me. This connection was publicised by the media, and the RFDS logos were prominently displayed on *Margery's* engine cowls. At every opportunity, I was only too happy to promote the excellent job the RFDS plays in its mission of serving rural Australia, and I trust that this exposure has been the catalyst for donations.

Although no formal fundraising campaign was mounted, a reasonable sum was raised during the course of the trip. This was supplemented by further donations as a result of talks given by me to various groups and associations following my return, and which continued for a few years.

Most of my audiences comprised men and women of around retirement age. The feedback from these people at the conclusion of my presentations was interesting, for nearly all of them could claim a connection, either directly or indirectly, with the Tiger Moth. They may themselves have flown the Tiger during the War period, or perhaps it was the experiences of a family member or close friend they wished to talk about. The stories they told were fascinating, and I never tired of hearing them.

One memorable talk I gave was to a group of eleven and twelve-year-old students from the Cooloongup Primary School, south of Perth. I was concerned about maintaining their interest during my presentation, which usually ran for an hour, including question time. To my surprise, they remained totally absorbed and asked an array of sensible questions at the conclusion. I was most impressed, and couldn't help but think that a seed might have been sown in one of these young minds to want to undertake an epic journey of their own one day. After all, they are the adventurers of the future.

*Margery* remained in England for a period of 15 months before being dismantled, packed into a container and shipped back to Perth. There she was reassembled, retaining her original trip livery. She now leads a quieter life stationed at either Jandakot, or our small farming property at York, named Woburn Field. From these locations we undertake local joy flights and the occasional fly-in or air show.

As a result of this, my Australia to England flight, I have been granted the following awards and records:

- Federation Aeronautique Internationale (FAI)
  (10 Inaugural World Records).

- Royal Federation of Aero Clubs of Australia
  (10 Inaugural Australian Records).

- Geoffrey de Havilland Trophy
  (Presented at the de Havilland Moth Club Annual Dinner, Woburn Abbey, England, 1998).

- Guinness World Record
  (Granted 21$^{st}$ February, 2000).

- Luskintyre Aviation Group Trophy
  "In recognition of being the first person to pilot a Tiger Moth from Australia to U.K. 1998." (Presented at Salute to Solo Aviators Dinner, June 1999).

- Olympic Torchbearer, Sydney 2000 Games.

# ACKNOWLEDGEMENTS

SPONSORS

- Malaysia Airlines
    - Accommodation in the South-East Asian cities of Bali, Surabaya, Jakarta, Penang, Phuket, Singapore, Bangkok and Karachi.
    - An airline ticket from London to Perth for the author.
- Mountain Designs - Perth
    - Cyclone, Windstopper jacket.
    - Gortex wet weather gear.
    - Thermal underwear.
    - Ski goggles and gloves.
- Skycraft Electronics
    - Installation Radio/GPS equipment.
    - Loan of hand-held GPS (back-up).
- Western Automotive
    - Leatherman tool.
    - Knee map holder.
    - Maps bag.
    - Flight ruler.
    - Torch.
- Champagne PC Services
    - Computer software for flight planning.
- Financial Sponsorships
    - Australian Geographic.
    - Insured at Lloyd's of London by Cox Aviation Insurance Services Ltd – arranged through Stirling Besso Ltd.

- June and John Brearley (sister and brother-in-law).
- Burns Sieber Chartered Accountants.
- Les, Pat and Peter Gunzburg.
- Old Wesley Collegians Association.
- Mobil (contribution towards oil).

## GENERAL

- Werner Buhlmann – Flight planning assistance and Planning Committee member.
- Brian Edwards – Loan of long-range fuel and oil tanks and general advice.
- Gerry Gannon – Chairman Planning Committee – Assistance with sponsorship, publicity and official departure from Langley Park.
- Murray Bow – Member Planning Committee.
- John Roberts – Assistance with computer flight planning, providing en route weather information and writing and distributing newsletter for duration of trip.
- Derek Leeder – Assistance with general information on Timor Sea crossing.
- Mike Rowe – Overflight International – Arranging overflight and landing clearances.
- John Fisher – Providing information on overseas consulates, landing points, safety equipment and other advice.
- Mike Vaisey and Paul Sharman – Vintage Engine Technology Ltd – Overhauling top half of engine, magnetos and carburettor.  Sponsoring hotel accommodation on arrival in Cambridge. Mike Vaisey – assistance with Tiger Moth/Gipsy Moth comparison details.
- RAAF – Loan of life-raft and providing training in its use.

- Tom Stephens – BHP (Troughton Island) – Approval to stay overnight – gratis.
- Fuel Suppliers
    - Vince Costello – Air-BP Paraburdoo.
    - Graham and Jan Lock – Mobil Port Hedland.
    - Bill Simons – Mobil Derby.
- RACWA – Hangar Staff
    - Glen Caple LAME – Chief Engineer – Overseeing preparation of *Margery* for flight.
    - Don Longville LAME – Engine and airframe work, maintenance training for periodic servicing, and putting together tool kit.
    - Viv Pavlich – significant airframe and systems work.
- Evelyn Brey – Secretary Dubai Flying Club U.A.E. – General assistance.
- Dr Will Reader and Ingrid Reader – Jeddah – Assistance with medical problem.
- Mike and Chantelle Gibbs – Auch, France – Accommodation and assistance with planning revised route – Auch to Abbeville.
- Stuart McKay MBE – Assistance with British Aerospace overweight approval and Cambridge arrival.
- Roger Morton – Publicity and newsletters.
- Jock Hay – Newsletters and Cambridge arrival.
- Cambridge Arrival
    - Mr Michael Marshall, CBE, DL, Chairman of Marshall of Cambridge (Holdings) Limited, and Vice Lord-Lieutenant of Cambridgeshire; and Terry Holloway, Group Support Executive of Marshalls – Permission to land at Cambridge and assistance with arrival function.
    - Hon. Clive Griffiths AO, JP, Agent General of the Government of Western Australia – Organised and sponsored arrival function.

- Dr Vivian Forbes – Associate Professor University of Western Australia, Curator of Maps – Assistance with technical map details.

- Carol (Wife) – For her love and support from the outset, including assistance with preparing maps and daily flight envelopes, and then continual moral support throughout the entire trip – until my arrival in England.

- Children – Campbell, Bradley, April and Alison for their love and ongoing support from the initial planning stages through to my arrival in England. Includes April providing additional route information and assisting with media enquiries at home and arranging spare parts for delivery to Bangkok and Dubai. Also providing updates of my progress to family and friends.

- Sunny Phegan (Secretary) – For her dedicated assistance with general planning for the trip and providing me with weather information, clearance details and general news en route. Providing updates of my progress to committee members, media and friends. Also for her patience and care in typing this manuscript in its many draft forms and assistance with proof reading.

**Note:** The entire manuscript and amendments were hand-written by the author.

- Rachel Brown  – Assistance with final drafts and proof reading.

- Bert Hingley – For his thorough editing of the manuscript, and the helpful advice and constructive criticism he provided.

# BIBLIOGRAPHY

BRAMSON, A.E. AND BIRCH, N.H.
*The Tiger Moth Story*,
AIRLIFE PUBLISHING LTD, ENGLAND. 1982.

CHICHESTER, SIR FRANCIS.
*The Lonely Sea and the Sky*,
PAN BOOKS LTD, LONDON. 1985.

COBHAM, K.B.E., SIR ALAN.
*Australia and Back*,
A. AND C. BLACK LTD, LONDON. 1926.

GWYN-JONES, T.
*Pioneer Aviator; The Remarkable Life of Lores Bonney*,
ST LUCIA. 1988.

LEWIS, J.M.
*Jimmy Woods, Flying Pioneer*,
FREMANTLE ARTS CENTRE PRESS,
FREMANTLE. 1989.

SHARP, C.M.
*DH A History of de Havilland*,
AIRLIFE PUBLISHING LTD, ENGLAND. 1982.

# Appendix 1

## B.H.A. MARKHAM
### ITINERARY AND FLIGHT SUMMARY – AUSTRALIA TO ENGLAND 1998

| DATE | DAY # | FROM | TO | DIST. NM | HOURS | REMARKS |
|---|---|---|---|---|---|---|
| April 26 | 1 | Jandakot | Geraldton | 200 | 3.1 | Via Langley Park, Perth (Landed) |
| April 27 | 2 | Geraldton | Paraburdoo | 378 | 5.4 | |
| April 28 | 3 | Paraburdoo | Pt. Hedland | 178 | 2.6 | |
| April 29 | 4 | Pt. Hedland | Derby | 350 | 5.5 | |
| April 30 | 5 | Derby | | | | Rest day |
| May 1 | 6 | Derby | Troughton Isl. | 263 | 4.3 | |
| May 2 | 7 | Troughton Island | Kupang | 258 | 3.2 | |
| May 3 | 8 | Kupang | Bali | 509 | 5.8 | Via Waingapu (Landed) |
| May 4 | 9 | Bali | Surabaya | 171 | 2.6 | |
| May 5 | 10 | Surabaya | Jakarta | 374 | 4.8 | |
| May 6 | 11 | Jakarta | Palembang | 238 | 4.7 | |
| May 7 | 12 | Palembang | Palembang | (240) | (4.1) | Turned back abm Berhala Island - storms Singapore Straits |
| | | Note: Distance and time not included in Summary Totals | | | | |
| May 7, 8 & 9 | 12-14 | | | | | Delayed 3 days Palembang by storms |
| May 10 | 15 | Palembang | Seletar (Singapore) | 266 | 4.2 | |
| May 11 | 16 | Seletar (Singapore) | | | | Rest day |
| May 12 | 17 | Seletar (Singapore) | Penang | 333 | 5.2 | |
| May 13 | 18 | Penang | Phuket | 217 | 3.0 | |
| May 14 | 19 | Phuket | Bangkok | 383 | 6.2 | |
| May 15 | 20 | Bangkok | | | | Rest day |
| May 16 | 21 | Bangkok | Yangon (Rangoon) | 332 | 5.4 | |
| May 17 | 22 | Yangon (Rangoon) | | | | Rest day |
| May 18 | 23 | Yangon (Rangoon) | Chittagong | 423 | 5.0 | Gwa and Sandoway (Overfly) |
| May 19-21 | 24-26 | Chittagong | | | | Held up by cyclone |
| May 22 | 27 | Chittagong | Calcutta | 188 | 3.2 | |
| May 23 | 28 | Calcutta | Jamshedpur | 127 | 2.4 | |

| Date | No. | From | To | NM | Hrs | Notes |
|---|---|---|---|---|---|---|
| May 24 | 29 | Jamshedpur | | | | Carried out 100 hourly service |
| May 25 | 30 | Jamshedpur | Nagpur | 413 | 6.5 | |
| May 26 | 31 | Nagpur | Ahmedabad | 382 | 5.8 | |
| May 27 | 32 | Ahmedabad | Karachi | 372 | 5.9 | |
| May 28 | 33 | Karachi | Gwadar | 263 | 5.0 | |
| May 29 | 34 | Gwadar | Dubai | 379 | 6.1 | |
| May 30 | 35 | Dubai | | | | Replace tacho and cable |
| May 31 | 36 | Dubai | | | | Rest day |
| June 1 | 37 | Dubai | Bahrain | 263 | 5.3 | |
| June 2 | 38 | Bahrain | Riyadh | 227 | 4.8 | |
| June 3 | 39 | Riyadh | | | | Rest day |
| June 4 | 40 | Riyadh | Jeddah | 462 | 8.2 | Repairs to alternator |
| June 5–10 | 41–46 | Jeddah | | | | |
| June 11 | 47 | Jeddah | Luxor | 427 | 7.3 | Via Cairo (Overfly) |
| June 12 | 48 | Luxor | Alexandria | 374 | 6.0 | |
| June 13 | 49 | Alexandria | Iraklion | 346 | 5.1 | |
| June 14 | 50 | Iraklion | Corfu | 373 | 5.2 | |
| June 15–17 | 51–53 | Corfu | | | | Repairs to wiring |
| June 18 | 54 | Corfu | Naples | 278 | 5.7 | Via Brindisi (Overfly) |
| June 19 | 55 | Naples | Cannes | 363 | 5.6 | Via Bastia/Poretta (Overfly) |
| June 20 | 56 | Cannes | Auch | 282 | 4.6 | Via Carcassone (Overfly) |
| June 21 | 57 | Auch | | | | Rest day |
| June 22 | 58 | Auch | Abbeville | 401 | 6.0 | Via Limoges (Overfly) |
| June 23 | 59 | Abbeville | | | | Delayed – poor weather Eng. Channel |
| June 24 | 60 | Abbeville | Cambridge | 158 | 2.6 | |
| Totals | | | | 10,951 | 172.3 | |

**Summary**

- **Total Distance** — 10, 951 NM (20, 281 km)
- **Total Flying time** — 10, 338 minutes or 172.3 hours
- **Average Speed** — 63.56 knots (10, 951 divided by 172.3) or 117.71 kph
- **Total Number of Days** — 60 days (35 flying days)

# Appendix 2

# FERRY FUEL/OIL TANKS

CASA AUSTRALIA
APPROVED SUPPLEMENT
APRIL 1998

ROYAL AERO CLUB OF WA
DE HAVILLAND DH-82A
FERRY FUEL SYSTEM

The ferry system also incorporates an auxiliary oil tank which is interconnected with the original oil tank. The purpose of this oil tank is to provide sufficient oil to the engine for the extended range.

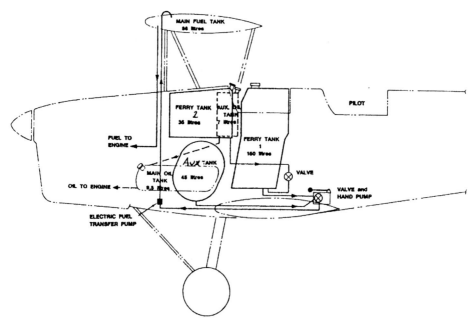

Courtesy Aeronautical Engineers Australia

# Appendix 3

# LUGGAGE AND EQUIPMENT

- Clothing – Flying suit, a few changes of light clothing plus thermal underwear, several pairs thick socks, jumper, Windstopper jacket, Gortex wet weather gear, scarf, gloves, cap and one pair spare shoes

- Tool kit – 26 tools plus small 12 piece socket set, torch and Leatherman knife

- Spares

| | |
|---|---|
| Exhaust gaskets x 4 | Fabric tape |
| Inlet gaskets x 4 | Insulation tape |
| Head gaskets x 2 | Lock wire |
| Rocker gaskets x 4 | Split pins – assorted |
| Rocker hat seals x 4 | Screws and nuts – assorted |
| Oil filter gasket x 1 | Washers – assorted |
| Exhaust nuts x 4 | General purpose grease |
| Access panels x 2 | Points grease – tube |
| Spark plugs x 4 | |

**Note:** Spare magnetos were not carried owing to *Margery's* magnetos being completely stripped and rebuilt prior to departure, i.e. they were in as new condition. Also saved weight.

- Liferaft/seat (Macchi jet type).

- Life jacket (helicopter type).

- Toilet bag.

- Medical kit.

- Sunscreen.

- Rations (biscuits and muesli bars).

- Water bottle (2 litre plastic cordial bottle with 2 foot plastic tube inserted).

- Camera – Canon A1 Sureshot 35mm (underwater type).

- Canvas bag (compact) containing maps, flight plans, general route information, flight planning equipment, log book, Maintenance Release and maintenance paperwork.

- Knee map holder.

- Town of Cambridge (WA) scroll to present to City of Cambridge UK.

- Canvas covers for cockpit, propeller and Pitot tube.

- Chocks (aluminium) and tie-down ropes.

- Bible.

- Diary.